OTHER TITLES OF INTEREST FROM ST. LUCIE PRESS

Leadership by Encouragement

Real Dream Teams

Problem Solving for Results

Focused Quality: Managing for Results

Mastering the Diversity Challenge: Easy On-the-Job Applications for Measurable Results

The Motivating Team Leader

Creating Productive Organizations: Manual and Facilitator's Guide

Organization Teams: Building Continuous Quality Improvement

Team Building: A Structured Learning Approach

Healthcare Teams: Building Continuous Quality Improvement

Creating Quality in the Classroom

Teams in Education: Creating an Integrated Approach

For more information about these titles call, fax or write:

St. Lucie Press
100 E. Linton Blvd., Suite 403B
Delray Beach, FL 33483
TEL (407) 274-9906 • FAX (407) 274-9927

$S{_L^t}$

D0182231

THE SKILLS
OF ENCOURAGEMENT

Bringing Out
the Best in Yourself
and Others

THE SKILLS OF ENCOURAGEMENT

Bringing Out the Best in Yourself and Others

Dr. Don Dinkmeyer
Dr. Lewis Losoncy

S^t_L

St. Lucie Press
Delray Beach, Florida

$S{}^t_L$

Published by
St. Lucie Press
100 E. Linton Blvd., Suite 403B
Delray Beach, FL 33483

Dedication

With love,
To my wife, Diane,
The shaper of the Losoncy culture

To our daughter Gabrielle,
Who says that worry simply means
It hurts in your imagination—imagine that!

To Tyler Baker,
Our momentum maker

To Lauren Losoncy,
More than a cousin, a role model

To Alexis Rae,
Gabby's very first best friend

Lew Losoncy

To Alfred Adler and Rudolf Drekurs,
Whose work stimulated
Our interest in encouragement

With love to my wife, E. Jane,
A continual source of encouragement

To my sons, Don Jr. and Jim,
Who have taken the concept of encouragement
And placed it at the center of
Their professional and family relationships

Don Dinkmeyer

Contents

Authors

Don Dinkmeyer, Ph.D., is President of Communication & Motivation Training Institute, Inc. in Coral Springs, Florida. He is a Diplomate in Counseling Psychology and a Diplomate in Family Psychology.

Dr. Dinkmeyer received the Professional Development Award from the American Association for Counseling and Development in 1986 and was named Distinguished Senior Contributor to Counseling Psychology by the American Psychological Association in 1990.

The author of over 150 professional articles and 30 books, Dr. Dinkmeyer has consulted and conducted workshops in 46 states, Canada, Mexico, South America, England, Germany, Switzerland, and Japan.

Lewis Losoncy, Ph.D., is a psychologist and the author of a dozen books on encouragement, motivation, teamwork, and success. His publications include *The Motivating Team Leader* and *Teamwork Makes the Dream Work.*

Dr. Losoncy is the psychologist for Matrix Essentials in Solon, Ohio, North America's largest producer of professional-only beauty products. He has been featured in various print media, from *Psychology Today* to *The Wall Street Journal,* and has appeared on CNN and CBS's "This Morning." Dr. Losoncy has lectured in all 50 states and many of Canadian provinces, as well as Australia and New Zealand.

1

Encouragement Is Positively The Way Up!

T he next time you are with a group of people, look for the encourager. He or she is the one whose arrival lights up the atmosphere, who circulates good news, who mobilizes the resources of each person, and who conveys that energy-giving optimism that raises the group "will" over the "won't." The encouraging person is buoyed up by the advantage of being positive, of being certain that life is worth living, that people would rather hope than despair, and that fear is the only enemy we face in life.

The antidote to fear is courage. And that courage is produced by encouragement.

Ultimately, the encouraging person's gift is a positive attitude coupled with the skills to encourage others to believe in themselves. This is a book about how to become an encourager to yourself and others. Perhaps there is no greater gift in life. And perhaps self-encouragement is the only skill you will ever need to put yourself into a positive state for the rest of your life.

Encouragement is positively the way up!

Who Were The Encouragers And Discouragers In Your Life?

Think for a moment. Can you recall a specific time when, as a young child, you worked hard to achieve a certain goal? Do you remember the feeling of satisfaction you experienced when you finally reached your goal? Who was the first person you wanted to tell about your success?

Now think about a time when you had a problem and needed to talk to someone. Who was the person you usually sought out to discuss your feelings with? Why did you choose that person? What did he or she do to help you? When we are "down in the dumps," some people always seem to have the talent to help us re-energize and move on to face our stresses, pressures, and the demands of life.

We call those positive people to whom we are attracted and with whom we share our interests *encouragers*. What makes encouragers so appealing to us? Are there common patterns that exist in most encouragers? To discover whether there are patterns in these effective people, we listened to many individuals, perhaps like you, talk about the encouraging people in their lives. Interestingly, encouragers exist in all walks of life. Some people chose parents, friends, teachers, supervisors, even hairdressers and police officers, as being the most encouraging to them. To better understand the specific skills of the encourager, we asked people to talk about the ingredients of their relationship with this influencing other person. Now let us ask you.

Take a moment to think about your relationship with your encouraging person. What was special about this relationship? How did you feel when you were with that person? Jot down your comments below.

We have listed some of what we feel are representative of the most frequently heard answers to this question. Do any of these observations match your response?

> "This person really listened and didn't immediately tell me I was wrong."

> "This person understood how I felt."

> "In this relationship I felt like a winner. I think this person felt that I was special, unique."

"I could be honest with this person and wouldn't have to be phony and didn't fear the results. I was even willing to be responsible for what I did if it were wrong."

I could disagree with this person and wasn't afraid of getting him or her angry."

"This person always had time for me."

"I felt safe with this person."

"This person always saw hope for me no matter how bad things seemed to be."

"This person had a good sense of humor."

"This person was enthusiastic about my experience."

"This person respected me for myself. The respect didn't come just because I got an A in school or did well, but just because I was me."

Are any of these comments similar to your response? If so, then your experience has been similar to that of many others, suggesting that perhaps there are common characteristics, or skills, that encouragers possess. We have heard many other answers to this same question, but the answers above were the most common.

Now, if you will, take a moment or two to think about the characteristics of the relationship between you and someone who was discouraging to you. Jot down your comments below.

Here are some of the comments people made concerning the characteristics of the most discouraging people in their lives:

"This person never listened to me when I talked and was always too busy."

"Nothing I could ever do was right, no matter how hard I tried. This person always expected perfection from me."

"This person would embarrass me. I felt constantly put down."

"This person only noticed my bad points."

"I was always scared around this person. The person was unpredictable."

Did any of your comments match the ingredients of these discouraging people? What additional responses would you add based on your own experiences?

By doing this simple exercise with people, it became clear to us that there were characteristics encouragers had that discouragers clearly lacked. An example is listening. Encouragers were described as people who listened without judging or condemning. Discouragers, contrarily, were described as people who were not effective listeners. From our information, then, we could theoretically range some behaviors of people from being totally discouraging to being totally encouraging to others. Let's consider a few characteristics:

Discouraging	Encouraging
Ineffective listening	Effective listening
Focuses on negatives	Focuses on positives
Competing, comparing	Cooperative
Threatening	Accepting
Uses sarcasm, embarrassment	Uses humor, hope
Humiliates	Stimulates
Recognizes only well-done tasks	Recognizes effort and improvement
Disinterested in feelings	Interested in feelings
Bases worth on performance	Bases worth on just being

Of course, we could go on looking at the skills of the encourager in terms of this polarity. Obviously, the totally discouraging or encouraging person does not exist. All of us, being human, have days when we are more or less effective at encouraging ourselves and others. Yet all of us do have the ability to move toward the more encouraging side of this chart.

Every time two people come in contact, both individuals are influenced to move in either a more "turned on," encouraged direction or in a "turned off," discouraged direction. When we are discouraged, we tend to discourage. And when we discourage others, we become more discouraged ourselves. By the same token, when we encourage someone else, we are encouraged as we realize the positive contribution we can make in helping others develop their "inner courage." This is contrary to the popular belief that the more we put other people down, the higher up we go. To contradict this belief in the seesaw effects of human relationships, many psychologists today even deal with depressed clients by recommending they do something to make someone else feel good. Apparently, when we extend ourselves in what Alfred Adler (1939) called "social interest," we become personally fulfilled.

Encouragement is the key ingredient in all positive personal and professional relationships. Did you ever have a doctor, for example, who was quite knowledgeable about medicine but had a poor, impersonal bedside manner? This doctor may have been quite insensitive to your world and experiences, and perhaps this created anxiety or tension on your part. All the knowledge in the world is ineffective in the hands of an insensitive person who lacks understanding of people.

Did you ever have a teacher whose brilliance was obvious but who was miles above and beyond the students? Perhaps you felt discouraged or intimidated. The end product was that you probably did not learn much, despite the fact that the teacher knew a lot. If you were like many other people, perhaps you even developed a dislike for the particular subject! Imagine if this individual had developed encouragement skills. Through an understanding of encouragement, this teacher would have shifted the focus from spouting facts to thirty uninvolved bodies to getting them to understand and feel excited about the subject.

Perhaps you have many examples from your everyday life to show how encouragement is a key to positive personal and professional relationships. The following model demonstrates the significance of encouragement:

Your Professional **Skills** (doctor, secretary, lawyer, teacher, nurse, etc.)	+	Your Encouragement **Skills** (communication, respect, attitude, etc.)	=	The Most Positive **You**

This model is relevant whenever two or more people meet. It matters not whether an individual is a salesperson, supervisor, teacher, or waiter. The skills of encouragement are the key factors that provide positive influences on effective relationships.

One wonders why the positive effects of encouragement have been so ignored in the past. The major reason, we believe, is that encouragement challenges a tradition that emphasized the use of power, competition, intimidation, and autocracy as a means to human relationships. Take a few moments to compare the effects of encouragement with the effects of intimidation.

A Positive Person Has An Optimistic View Of Our Possibilities For Change

Recently, a great deal of interest and excitement has centered on ways of improving our skills in motivating ourselves and others to a fuller development of talents and resources. Pessimistic notions that people cannot change and are doomed by their childhood experiences are giving way to the more optimistic ideas as first advanced by Alfred Adler. Adler suggested that neither heredity nor environment is the ultimate determinant of personality, but that each only provides the basic building blocks out of which we construct the kind of person we want to be (Ansbacher and Ansbacher, 1956).

We agree with Adler that people have the capacity for constructive change in their lives. We also believe, as Adler did, that this change is more likely to occur in a relationship with a person who is encouraging.

This interest in helping people grow and reach a fuller development of their resources is visible everywhere today. Parents, for example, concerned about their discouraged or irresponsible child, frequently find themselves exhausted in trying to find ways to help their loved one. Educators, faced with vast underuse of student potential as reflected in declining test scores, poor attendance, disinterest, and boredom, seek ways of motivating the disinterested student in more positive directions. Business and industry personnel, aware of the effects of worker alienation, job apathy, and active and passive rebellion, spend millions annually to shift this costly trend. Very simply put, the world is looking for positive people who bring out the best in others—people who are encouraging.

Goals Of Encouragement

People who are unhappy, depressed, anxious, angry, or even unproductive are not disturbed; rather, they are discouraged. They lack courage in their ability to grow and take risks in more self-fulfilling directions. This immobilization, fear of failure, or negative goal seeking is reflected in a lifestyle overwhelmed with a theme of "I can't change."

Encouragement is the process of facilitating the development of a person's inner resources and courage toward positive movement. The encouraging person helps the discouraged person remove some of the self-imposed attitudinal roadblocks. The goal of encouragement then is to aid the individual to move from a philosophy that suggests "I can't" to the more productive "I will" in order to help people find their own "personal power." This change is demonstrated on the Courage Direction Chart developed by Losoncy (1980) (see table below). With increasing courage, the individual starts to move from left to right.

Given this new personal power, the encouraged person looks at life out of new spectacles. These new spectacles focus on the opportunities in life as opposed to the fear of change.

The positive, courageous person's level of courage increases as he or she moves from the beliefs on the left to the beliefs on the right in the following table.

Courage Is Movement Toward

"TURNED OFF"			"TURNED ON"
From:		**To:**	
I *can't* make an effort	I won't make an effort	I *can* make an effort	I *will and am making* an effort
Constricted	Responsible, but no movement	Responsible, hope, possibilities of movement	Construction
Desire for mastery of sameness	Passive resistance	Attitude growth	Desire for mastery of newness (courage of imperfection)
Stagnated			Growing
Irresponsible			Responsible
Helpless			Significant
Opinionated			Flexible
Energy misdirected			Energy directed toward goals

Overview Of The Book

This is a book about becoming a positive person through encouragement. We believe that this process is not a mysterious one, but rather is quite similar to developing skills in any area. For example, what makes a good dancer? A good dancer has a great deal of knowledge about dancing, a positive attitude toward dancing, and well-developed skills in dancing. Similarly, the encouraging person has knowledge about encouragement, a positive attitude toward life, and skills in encouraging.

Many potentially positive students are frustrated in their attempts to be encouraging and find no concrete starting point. Operationally, it means very little when someone says, "use encouragement." Consequently, we have chosen to focus on specific skills. These skills of encouragement can be learned on a step-by-step basis and later put together as a whole. We begin the journey to become a positive person by understanding the psychology of encouragement.

References

Adler, Alfred. *Social Interest.* New York: Putnam, 1939.

Ansbacher, H. and Rowena Ansbacher. *The Individual Psychology of Alfred Adler.* New York: Basic Books, 1956.

Losoncy, Lewis. *You Can Do It.* New York: Simon & Schuster, 1980.

2

The Psychology Of Encouragement

You may often be confused by the way people behave. Your spouse goes on what seems to you to be a spending spree. It makes no sense to you. You have a very tight budget and unnecessary things are being bought. Your son knows the importance of keeping things orderly around the house and being on time for his appointments. However, he is often late and calls on you to bail him out. You say, "I've told you a thousand times..." There are countless additional examples of behavior that seems to make no sense.

The reason behavior doesn't make sense is because perhaps you are limited by your understanding of human behavior. You don't have an effective theory which enables you not only to understand but to predict why you do what you do and why others do what they do.

Sue has a son, Jack, 15 years old. Jack has considerable athletic ability in several sports and also demonstrated academic skills when he was in elementary school. However, he has withdrawn from sports and is currently failing in most of his subjects. Sue has resorted to all the traditional corrective measures such as pushing, prodding, and cajoling, all to no avail.

What might be the purpose of this sudden change in Jack's behavior? Why is he no longer functioning effectively?

What kind of tension and involvement is he getting from Sue?

In this chapter, you will learn to become a more effective encourager by understanding a theory of human behavior that describes the purpose or nature of behavior, the significance of belonging, and guidelines for more effective relationships with all people.

Jack and Lynda have three children. Their oldest teenage son is athletic, but he is shy and lacks self-confidence. They decide he needs help in making more friends, increasing his scholastic average, and becoming more successful in athletics. They attempt to motivate him by trying to find some activity in which he would be recognized as outstanding. They believe this would help him become more outgoing, popular, and involved with people. This is an example of the parents' good intentions but faulty methods. They would like to improve their son's self-confidence, but it is likely he will feel he is worthwhile and acceptable only if he is very special.

To become more encouraging, Jack and Lynda need to help their son by changing their point of view and recognizing that he is probably doing his best and may be limited by feelings of inadequacy. It would be more helpful to recognize any attempt, progress, or positive effort he makes. The task is to stimulate his courage and his willingness to try things—to recognize any effort, even in small increments of progress.

When you are puzzled about a person's behavior or your relationship, how do you find a way to understand and change what you are experiencing? Do you attack the other person's behavior and beliefs? Do you decide this is just another example of your inability to relate to people? Do you feel guilty?

To be an encouraging person, it is essential that you have meaningful and effective beliefs and ideas about human behavior. Without basic beliefs, you tend to react to behavior instead of respond. You see it and react. Reacting is automatic, with no flexibility. There is no decision or choice.

Responding to behavior involves considering possible ways to respond and then taking action to create the best solution for all concerned.

To be an encourager, you need to understand the purpose of behavior. We can only become more encouraging as we learn to understand why people behave the way they do. Encouragement then becomes a method for motivating people.

Motivation, from our point of view, is understanding the reason for the behavior. Behavior makes sense to the person behaving. We need to understand the behavior from that person's perception or point of view.

If you understand behavior in terms of cause, you are concerned with what caused a particular action instead of the purpose of the action. If you take the casual approach and believe situations are the result of events, then you believe you can predict how a person will behave.

Behavior has a purpose. It is self-determined and chosen instead of just influenced by some event beyond our control. We choose to decide and move in the direction of our purposes and goals.

Goals give direction and become the basis for final explanation or behavior. What you are seeking or attempting to achieve explains why you are behaving in a way that may not make sense to others but makes sense to you in light of your goals. While you may not always be aware of your goals, they are created, chosen, or decided upon by you, and they give direction to all of your relationships. As you begin to understand the significance of the purpose of behavior, you will ask, "for what purpose?"

Bill is in his junior year of high school and has previously done quite well in school. His parents are hoping he will enroll in a pre-med program, but Bill has relatively little interest in this type of study.

As he comes to the end of the first grading period, Bill has accumulated three F's and two D's. His parents and teachers are shocked. His teachers say he is a bright boy and has a lot of ability, but he just doesn't seem to get things handed in. He also resists any of the extra projects that are available. His parents are extremely discouraged. They tell Bill that his behavior just doesn't make sense. If he does this poorly, he will find it difficult to get into a good school.

Does this behavior make sense to Bill? It makes sense to him because he has no interest in enrolling in a pre-med course at a major institution. His interests lie more in technical work, computers, or TV repair. If he fails to qualify for college, he will be in a position where he can make a decision in line with his interests. His behavior makes sense to him even if it does not to others.

All Behavior Has Social Meaning

Human behavior is social behavior and it is influenced by our relationships with others. Behavior helps you find a place and maintain certain social goals. Whenever behavior appears confusing and you can't understand why a person is acting in a certain manner, you can look for the social meaning in the behavior.

Gwen is very concerned that Dave and Greg, her sons, are dressed properly for church. Although they belong to a congregation where the style of attire is informal, every Sunday morning she goes through the routine of closely inspecting all details of the boys' clothing. Her husband, Jack, is totally confused by this push for perfection and is aggravated because Gwen attempts to apply the same standards to him.

If Jack is to feel less discouraged and find a way to relate more meaningfully to Gwen about this, he must understand her behavior. Gwen believes that others (the pastor, her parents, people in the congregation) expect respectful dress. The social meaning of her behavior is, "I am acceptable when I do what others expect; if I don't do what others expect, I will be rejected." Based on this perception of life, it makes sense for Gwen to attempt to control the dress standards of the boys and Jack. However, if she were to realize that she is already acceptable and cannot increase her acceptability by enforcing this fictional dress code, then she would be able to create a better family attitude toward church.

Belonging Is A Basic Goal

We all have the desire to belong to someone or something. Belonging may be as important as working for a worthy cause. Our social institutions develop and continue on the basis of this widely accepted goal. If you look at the local and national community and observe the continuous proliferation of social and service organizations, you can see how the goal of belonging stimulates the growth of such organizations. New organizations will be developed as long as people have the need to belong.

The American professional and amateur sports scene is testimony to the interest in identifying with and belonging to a cause. For some people, their worth is based on being affiliated with winners instead of losers.

At an early age, children begin to show this goal of belonging as they identify with TV programs and advertised brand names. Adolescents are even more involved and have an even more intense need to belong to their peer group; they identify through music, clothing, hairstyles, etc. How would you complete the following statement?

I am only worthwhile if I belong to:

People believe they are as fulfilled, valued, or self-actualized insofar as they have a feeling of belonging. Self-acceptance and acceptance of others emerge from social interest, willingness to participate in the give and take of life, and the desire to identify with others.

Actually, you move toward greater mental health as you exercise social interest. The more people you are concerned about, the more positive are your feelings about yourself. As you learn to cooperate, you are free of fear and anxiety and feel more confident.

Bill is very active in his company and can be counted on to contribute to or participate in any worthwhile cause. He is also active in his church study group and social groups. Everyone knows Bill can be counted on to pitch in. Bill finds his meaning and place in life through contributing. He believes he is somebody when he belongs and is contributing and feels he is not worthwhile if he is not involved and contributing.

To encourage a person, you must learn the ways in which they feel accepted. People can only get a feeling of acceptance by belonging to something they value.

Personality Has Unity And Pattern

The unity and pattern in our lifestyle is expressed through our actions and attitudes. Your pattern of behavior is predictable. Your behavior and psychological movement are direct expressions of your beliefs and goals. Although a goal may not be in your awareness, you do what you intend. A basic part of understanding behavior is learning to understand and trust psychological movement. What a person does, as opposed to his or her words, reveals that person's purpose or goal. Watch a person's feet instead of only hearing his or her words.

Bob has been selling for the same company for eight years. He always has high hopes at the start of a new product season, which he communicates to his sales manager. However, he finds it difficult to get started in the morning and is often late for his calls. He also gets involved in a lot of small talk, which delays him from making some calls each day. He characteristically says, "I've got to get started earlier tomorrow and cut the small talk," but things just don't change. Bob is getting discouraged about his progress, as are his wife and his sales manager.

This is a classic case of good intentions without results. If you are going to encourage Bob to change, you must begin by recognizing that the purpose of his being tardy and wasting his time is probably not a conscious goal. He may unconsciously fear success and the expectations he believes others have of him. Rather than succeed and be expected to live up to his success, Bob chooses the route of procrastination.

If Bob can learn to accept himself as he is, and not have high expectations for himself, he will no longer be setting up his own stumbling blocks. With realistic goals to pursue, and with a belief that he is not just what he produces in sales but a person of value, Bob could be free to have a healthier approach to his work.

Behavior Has A Purpose

All of our psychological movement is pulled by a specific purpose or goal. This is contrary to the belief that behavior is taught. Human behavior is far more than the result of a cause. We choose, decide, and then move in the direction of our goals. Goals are the final cause or explanation of behavior. The goal in itself tells us the why or the reason for the behavior.

Ralph is 16 and in his sophomore year of high school. He does just average work in most classes but very well in social studies. Test scores indicate he could be an outstanding student, but he makes minimal efforts academically. His parents are concerned and set up a system of rewards for performance. They are dismayed to find that Ralph does not respond. His father has tried to get him involved in athletics, but Ralph always demonstrates his lack of ability and his father has given up. Socially, Ralph has limited contacts. His peers all know him and are friendly, but Ralph doesn't extend himself and has no close friends. His mother has tried to stimulate his latent musical ability, and although Ralph has been willing to take lessons, he doesn't apply himself.

Ralph shows many signs of discouragement. Both the open and subtle expectations of his parents and teachers have been rejected, and high standards as perceived by him are unreachable. Hence, he makes no effort. His goal is to display his inability in order to be excused from functioning. If he shows he cannot get good grades or perform athletically, musically, or socially, Ralph will eventually be excused from functioning.

In order to encourage Ralph, one must begin by helping him develop self-confidence. This involves communicating that performing at an average level academically is acceptable. There should be no open or subtle demands to be more productive. It is only as Ralph comes to feel he can be accepted for what he is, and he is acceptable even though the product (grades) may not be, that he can begin to generate the self-confidence necessary to believe in himself and function more comfortably.

Too often, we confuse the product and the person. You usually are doing the best you can at the moment. The product, if compared with other products, may be unacceptable, but that doesn't make you unacceptable. This message has to be communicated clearly if you are to live courageously and enjoy your resources.

Karen is in charge of the secretarial pool. She takes her assignment very seriously and wants to make sure that everybody is doing their full share of the work. When Janet appears to be taking more time than Karen believes necessary for a particular job, Karen tells Janet she must increase her rate of production. Janet, challenged by Karen's type of supervision, decides to do her best at her own pace and not be concerned with Karen's comments. When Karen persists in trying to get Janet to do more, Janet decides to slow down.

Here we have all the evidence of a power struggle. Karen believes you can get people to cooperate by close supervision and force, but Janet refuses to be forced; hence the impasse. If Karen's task is to ensure productivity, she might give more attention to noting what Janet does that is acceptable and comment on that. Once the power struggle is launched, Karen needs to be aware that she must pull out of the power contest, because there is no way to win in the long run by domination. Developing an accepting, cooperative atmosphere in which people are concerned with contributing to the common good will be much more satisfying for all concerned.

Striving For Significance Explains Motivation

We are all concerned with our reputation, which is the way in which we are known and how people see and understand us. Psychologists refer to this as *the basic striving for significance and recognition.* We are concerned with moving from an inferior or less significant position to one in which we are recognized and valued. This striving for significance can lead to overcompensation. The goal of striving for significance is power, special attention, or recognition for our uniqueness.

George believes that if he can't be the best, he will show he can be the worst, most difficult child to deal with. This forces others to deal with him accordingly. Feeling he has no chance to be the best and recognized on the useful side of life, he shifts to the useless side through misbehavior, delinquency, and drug use.

The individual who feels encouraged by others seeks significance by contributing, being responsible, cooperating, and refusing to become involved in conflicts. The choice of how one becomes known or significant is up to the individual. The person who is able to encourage others and feels encouraged will choose the active–constructive route.

Kevin is a fine tennis player and golfer. He is well known at his country club as the top tennis player and one of the best golfers in the area. His recognition and significance come from his reputation as an athlete. He does not believe in his abilities to socialize and make friends and hence is reserved and not sought out socially.

Kevin's athletic abilities have created an image of superiority which Kevin believes he must live up to. Since his worth and value have been established by being superior and better than others, Kevin has confused being valued and accepted with being special and first. In order to encourage Kevin socially, it will be necessary to accept him as a person and to identify and value any social resource he may have (interest in others, a warm smile, or good listening ability). He may be helped to recognize that one can be worthwhile and acceptable without being the most popular or the social leader of the group.

Behavior Is A Function Of Perception

The most effective understanding of behavior comes through an understanding of how the individual perceives the world. The perception includes not just the individual's vision, but the individual meaning given to all that is perceived. Perception is the event plus the individual meaning or interpretation of the event. Your behavior is always influenced not just by the event but by your unique interpretation of that event.

It isn't the neighbor's response to your barking dog but how you interpret his feelings and beliefs about your dog which concerns you. If you believe your neighbor is angry, you respond to *your* perception, even though your neighbor may merely be annoyed and believe you are careless. (It's major to you, but minor to your neighbor—people perceive things differently.) Thus, you make an inappropriate response, which could have been avoided had you listened more carefully to your neighbor's feelings and beliefs. When you comprehend the individual's private logic, you can be more encouraging.

Jack is a professor at the local university and is respected in his field. He is a good teacher and enjoys interacting with his students. Everything would appear to be satisfactory, but Jack finds his work difficult. The dean of his area attempts to control the staff, but Jack is not willing to be controlled. As a result, Jack is given meager raises, assignments, and responsibilities, which he finds unfair. It is obvious the dean is out to win.

Jack perceives the situation at the university as a power contest. After attempting to fight it for a while, he finally withdraws from the struggle to find a position without the harassment. Jack finally resigns his position and accepts a job as a consultant in industry, where his skills are respected and he is well received.

The Psychology Of Use Versus The Psychology Of Possession

The psychology of use means how you decide to use what you have. The psychology of possession is an inventory of what you have, but it doesn't tell how you have decided to use what you have. It doesn't matter what you have, but it does matter what you do with what you have.

The abilities and potential you possess are less important than what you decide to do with them. How you choose to make use of your talents or environment is more important than your potential (the abilities you have).

Often an individual appears to have considerable intellectual capability, unusually fine physical coordination, or talent in an area such as art or music, but doesn't choose to use it. For some reason, the individual has decided it doesn't pay to use the ability.

There is a difference between what you have and how you use it. You have freedom of choice not to use your potential. One often hears, "He has great potential, but we can't get him to use it." Understanding that all behavior has a purpose and giving a person the power to choose is the most effective way to stimulate someone's development.

Optimism

Optimism is a sign of power and potential. To be effective you need to focus on the potential good that is everywhere. At times you may become over-concerned with what doesn't work, or the down side. Fears and limitations become all-encompassing. Gray skies don't reveal the rainbow and the hope that exist.

Martin Seligman, in his book *Learned Optimism* (1991), has developed the scientific basis for optimism. You can either be pessimistic, discouraged, and helpless or you can be optimistic, positive, courageous, and seek solutions. The choice is up to you.

As Seligman indicates, there are three crucial dimensions to your explanatory style: permanence, pervasiveness, and personalization. These become beliefs which direct your behavior. Permanence is the belief that things which cause negative or bad events in life are permanent. "There's nothing I can do. I am helpless." Events are seen in terms of always and never, permanent, and pessimistic.

The optimistic, courageous person has a certainty that no problem is permanent and things *will* change. "I can find a way through this." Optimists see the good events in their lives as related to their positive traits and abilities and not to their moods or feelings.

Pervasiveness—This is a tendency to catastrophize. If one thing isn't working, other things aren't working. Soon the negativism has spread like the plague.

Positive people make specific explanations and don't generalize the bad to everything in their lives. Negative beliefs are challenged. They don't see themselves as the problem but believe they are responsible for changing the situation.

Personalization—When bad things happen, you blame yourself. Externalizing is blaming other people and circumstances. Internalizing is self-blame and results in reduced self-esteem. People who blame external events tend to like themselves more than those who blame themselves.

You have a choice about what you believe and can develop positive expectations. To help you find solutions and options when there are challenges, check whether you are personalizing, believing they are permanent or pervasive. Challenge these beliefs and identify the perceptual alternative—the positive potential in what appears to be negative.

To put these ideas into action, do the following:

- Make a list of your beliefs that help make things work for you.

- Post your list of beliefs somewhere where you can remind yourself of your effectiveness.

- List your limiting beliefs.

- Identify the fallacies and mistakes in these beliefs.

You will be further developing your optimism skills in Chapter 16.

Encouragement Skills

An essential encouragement skill is to be able to identify the goals or purposes of behavior. These goals may take the form of attention, power, revenge, or the display of inadequacy. You can learn to identify the goal by being in touch with the feelings you experience in a situation. For example, if you are feeling merely annoyed, the goal is probably getting attention. If you are feeling angry, the goal is probably power. If you are feeling hurt, this is an indicator that the goal is revenge. If you feel you want to give up, the goal may be to display inadequacy and be excused.

Your ability to identify the goal comes from your understanding of the various purposes of behavior. Determine the goal of specific misbehavior and the feelings you experience when that misbehavior occurs.

Application Of Identifying The Purpose Of Behavior

Think of a situation either at home or work when there was a lack of cooperation or resistance to your request. Identify what the person was doing, how you were feeling when this occurred, and what your typical response was. Identify from this sequence what may have been the purpose of the misbehavior.

To summarize:

1. Identify a situation.

2. Explain the behavior of both the other person and yourself.

3. Identify your feelings about this person's behavior.

4. Recall your typical response to the person's behavior.

5. Detect the goal of the misbehavior.

Reference

Seligman, Martin. *Learned Optimism*. New York: Knopf, 1991.

3

Getting High
On Yourself Skills

nventory has a variety of meanings depending upon
the kind of work you do or the way you keep track of
things around your house. Taking an inventory usually
involves a careful audit of all the things owned by the
business of which you are a part or your personal
possessions.

When you move, you obviously take a careful inventory of what you give to the movers. When you send
important documents, you take a careful inventory of what
is being sent. When you take these inventories, you are
making sure you are taking account of everything you
have.

We believe it is important that you take a "self-inventory." This inventory will help you to identify your strengths,
your resources, and your potential. It will give you a good
analysis of your strengths.

Some of us are more skilled at quickly identifying our
limitations, liabilities, and deficits. We can identify how
we are not as attractive as others, not as strong, not as
skilled, not as witty, not as outgoing, etc. When we come
to the positive side of our inventory, we are sometimes
very modest in sharing our strengths.

Jack was let go by a major corporation as part of a
reorganization to reduce the work force dramatically. At
first, he was discouraged and disappointed because he
had worked for this corporation for over twenty-five years.
His plans were to finish his work career with the same
corporation. Now he is "on the street" looking for a new
position.

He has decided that in order to be effective in selling himself in the job market or becoming an entrepreneur on his own, he needs to assess his strengths and talents. As he writes down his strengths, he identifies some he knows he has been using and others that have been "on hold." He is good at listening to others and communicating back what he has heard. He is encouraging and can find out what is good in another person. He tries to pull people together by identifying their similarities instead of their differences. He is always able to see a positive alternative to any situation.

Armed with this new appraisal of himself, he obviously is in a better position to start to look into his possibilities in the work force.

If you are basing your happiness and success on the actions of other people, you are sentencing yourself to a frustration that will last as long as you wait for others to change. There is a better way to become a positive person. There is something that you can do now, instead of passively waiting. The route to becoming a positive person and developing the skills of encouragement must first go through the process of personal development and self-encouragement. Self-help books often talk about ways to change other people. In the encouragement process, we believe it is essential to begin by developing your own encouraging perspective. You recognize that you cannot encourage others unless you first have internalized an encouraging approach to life. As you decide on an attitude that is positive and courageous, you empower yourself to receive all the benefits of the encouraged state.

Many of us recall the song "You Light Up My Life." This chapter focuses on "*I* Light Up My Life." This is not an egotistic, self-sufficient approach; it simply says that the responsibility for lighting up your life belongs to you and not others. You neither blame nor demand that others create joy and happiness for you.

Getting high has become associated with using various substances such as alcohol, drugs, or prescribed medications. Personal power, excitement, thrills, conquests, and manipulation are also sources of getting high.

The high we are advocating is the natural high which was first set forth by Dr. Walter (Buzz) O'Connell. The formula for the natural high is NH = SE + SI + SH. The symbols indicate that NH (natural high) is based upon SE (self-esteem)—feeling one's worth and value—plus SI (social interest)—the ability to cooperate, give and take, and work with others—and SH (sense of humor)—the ability to see things in perspective (O'Connell, 1975).

The only absolute control you have in your life is your ability to expand or constrict your self-esteem, your social interest, and your sense of humor. You have this control only when you believe you have such control and exercise it. This changes you from someone who is fault-finding and blaming to a person who recognizes that you have the ability to change a situation.

The positive person has self-esteem. This includes a sense of personal effectiveness and personal worth. You know your capabilities and how to apply them in various situations in life. You have the courage to be imperfect. You can make a mistake and try again. You can attempt something you aren't sure will be successful. You don't fear and avoid perceived limitations.

You focus on and own your resources. You could be a "can opener," in that you believe you *can* instead of offering a litany of excuses why you can't. You have self-respect and confidence. This acceptance and courage is empowering.

A Self-Inventory

One of the ways to both access and build your self-esteem is to take an inventory of your strengths, assets, resources, and potential. The following questions will help you begin your self-inventory.

1. Identify and recognize your claim to fame. What is it you do well? Comparison is with yourself and not with other people. (For example, "I'm a good basketball player.") You are only

identifying your traits; you are not comparing yourself with others. One of the things that often limits your ability to function is your focus on how you compare with others. You may think that if you aren't first or best, then you are worst or inadequate.

2. List three to five things you like or appreciate about yourself. You may find it easier to list a number of things you don't like about yourself, but ignore that temptation.

3. What is new and good in your life? If you can't identify anything, what would be new and good in your life if you had a more positive outlook? Change your perception by being optimistic.

4. What are three to five things you *regularly* do that you enjoy? This may help you become more aware of why your life is more or less enjoyable than you'd like. (Are the stumbling blocks to getting high on yourself the ways in which you limit your joy?)

5. How do you show you are taking personal responsibility for your life? How often do you say, "I should" or "I have to" instead of "I choose to"?

Self-esteem, social interest, and a sense of humor are all products of what you think about yourself.

Sue, who is 24, has deep feelings of inadequacy. These feelings often result in depression and deep discouragement. When she surveys the various challenges of living, she sees few places, in her opinion, where she is successful. She has a very modest clerical job, although she is a junior college graduate. She has few girlfriends and few boyfriends. She is an attractive woman, but because she doesn't believe it, she sees all the places in which she is making mistakes and failing to succeed.

In the process of counseling, Sue became more aware of her worth and identified things she liked about herself. She developed activities and hobbies she regularly could enjoy. Over a period of time, she made some of the following decisions. She changed her wardrobe and hairstyle and joined social groups where she became friends with both men and women.

As she changed the way in which she saw herself and her relationships, she changed the things she had been complaining about.

She helped to change herself through self-affirmation. Self-affirmation is based upon total, unconditional self-acceptance. It excludes any negative self-talk and instead self-affirms the individual by recognizing positive things, i.e., "I am capable," "I am worthwhile," "I relate effectively with people."

What are some of the ways you could begin to affirm yourself? Discouragement can be a major block in affirming and getting high on yourself. Discouragement is a result of high standards which help you feel you are not quite enough.

- **Over-ambition**—Always wanting to be a little more

- **Pessimism**—Feeling it is not going to work anyhow

- **Comparisons**—Comparing yourself with those who are better than you

Discouragers are critical, fault-finding, pessimistic people who regularly supply you with put-downs and negative comments. The put-downs are designed to make the discourager feel better by making you feel less. Discouragers can be likened to vultures who attempt to take the vitality and energy from your life. One of the essential factors in building your self-esteem and natural high is to avoid discouraging experiences at work, school, and in your social life. Recognize that some of your discouraging experiences are the result of choices you made about how and when to compete.

Bringing about this change involves developing courage. Courage includes an active, social interest. It is based upon a recognition that others are at least as important as you are and that one of your goals in life is to be actively involved in assisting others.

Social interest is the capacity to give and take. Courage helps energize and strengthens your route to acquiring a natural high.

Courage also involves practicing new responses. You know your typical response to a request at work when you are asked to do something. Knowing your typical response, try doing exactly the opposite. You'll surprise yourself. You'll take one more step on the route to your NH. Become a possibility thinker instead of one who always sees danger and disaster lurking around the corner. Recognize that every situation has a solution, although it may not be a perfect one.

Courage and fear are interrelated. They both have a lot to do with your progress. The only difference between courage and fear is the direction of the movement. Courage moves in a positive direction. It is a plus. It gets you somewhere. Fear is negative movement. It is a minus and it leaves you discouraged.

Some perceptions that keep you from realizing your potential for growth and development include the following mistaken ones. Each begins with the same introductory phrase.

1. When I am approved of by others, I...

2. When I am in complete control, I...

3. When I am intellectually superior and right, I...

4. When I am being taken care of by others, I...

5. When I am morally superior, I...

If any of these five stumbling blocks are part of your perceptions, you have a good idea of what is keeping you from making progress. Mistaken perceptions, or faulty ideas, are self-created stumbling blocks to keep you from moving forward. For example, it would be nice to be approved of, but it is neither essential nor required. No one ever achieves complete control.

The Natural High Levels

A natural high helps you become a positive person. The levels of the natural high move you toward increasing your self-worth and self-esteem.

Natural High: Level 1

You are able to be in touch with all of your resources and feel good about yourself. You have no need to compare and compete with others. You are free from self-constrictions.

You are your own boa (belief or attitude) constrictor. Your beliefs and attitudes keep you from functioning more effectively. They create a competitive power-seeking world, which makes demands on you. As you remove the constrictions of "shoulds," self-judgments, and blame, you are free to become more of a friend to yourself. You encourage, support, accept, affirm, and believe in yourself. You have the courage to be imperfect. You have a concern for others. You aren't on a self-escalator that attempts to take you above others. You work to be on an equal plane with others instead of a vertical plane. You are far less focused on striving for perfection. You focus more on being useful than on being more than others.

You now see mistakes as only a way to help you grow and learn. You expect you will make mistakes and don't get upset about them.

Natural High: Level 2

You are learning to be more in control of your self-esteem. You aren't concerned about having power over people. You become an encourager who focuses on the resources of others and helps build their self-confidence and self-worth.

The Skills And Process Of Getting High On Yourself

1. Listen and attend to others. When you are in contact with them, stop your preoccupation with what you are doing. Listen and be in a position to hear the whole message.

2. Before you talk with others, clarify the message they have sent to you. "I hear what you are saying, feeling, etc."

3. Use put-ups instead of put-downs. What are some things you could do to help build the other person's self-esteem? What could you say that is positive?

4. Respond reflectively, while continuing to stay with the other person's feelings.

5. Look for similarities. What do the two of you have in common? Where are some places you can universalize?

6. Give them feedback on how they are coming across to you.

7. Encourage them for their strengths and not their perfections.

8. Help them to see perceptual alternatives, or more positive, effective ways they can look at the world.

Natural High: Level 3

In this advanced state, harmony occurs between you and your self-concept. You respect yourself and are self-appreciative. At this level, you attempt to become more free of your roles, goals, and controls. You work instead on certain skills:

• Meditation

• Self-hypnosis

• Relaxation

• Guided imagery

• Humor—not taking yourself so seriously, not getting involved with putting yourself down

• Not needing to compare

It is clear that no one can create this natural high without a well-developed sense of humor.

Application Of Getting High On Yourself Skills

Your only absolute control in life is your ability to expand or constrict your self-esteem. There are systematic ways to expand your self-esteem. You can do this by identifying your strengths, listing them, and appreciating them. You can also do this by daily affirmations that are personal and positive. Complete the following statement with a positive affirmation:

I am...

Then do five affirmations.

When you feel discouraged, what are the specific factors involved in the discouragement?

How do courage and fear influence your progress?

_____

Reference

O'Connell, Walter. *Action Therapy & Adlerian Theory*. Chicago, IL: Alfred Adler Institute of Chicago, 1975.

4 Listening Builds Relationships

D onna is a sensitive and compassionate listener. She would rather listen to what you are saying than attempt to tell you her problems or give you instant solutions to yours. She pays careful attention to what is said and what is not said. She listens carefully to identify the feelings behind as well as the full meaning of the message.

A friend who has just come from the doctor's office visits Donna. She learned she has a serious medical problem and is frightened about her future. Donna listens and responds to her friend's feelings by saying, "You're very upset, scared, and worried." She stays with her friend's feelings and helps her friend start to see possible alternatives.

Donna encourages regularly through the process of being an encouraging, attentive listener. If you have such a person, whether in your spouse, colleagues at work, or friends, know what a valuable person you have to confide in.

An accepting and understanding relationship is the foundation that nurtures encouragement. Unless there is an atmosphere of acceptance, respect, and understanding, it is unlikely that encouragement will occur. However, when the discouraged person feels heard, understood, and respected, this already is encouraging.

Listening is basic to all communication and the encouragement process. When you listen, you show value and seek to support and understand the other person. This begins the process of encouragement.

Listening involves giving your full attention to the person you are with. It involves hearing not only the content but the feelings, beliefs, and attitudes. The skilled listener then moves to communicating the beliefs, feelings, and attitudes that he or she is hearing. Through the simple process of listening, being heard, and processing feedback, the other person starts to feel encouraged and valued.

Sue has been active in her neighborhood, working with children as well as senior citizens. A new community is being built close to her home. She feels threatened by the proximity of the building as well as the rumors that the residents will be an ethnic group. Feeling threatened, she communicates this to members of a church group active in developing and supporting this community. They are shocked and angered by her attitude. Sue feels rejected and disappointed and wants to withdraw.

What has happened in this exchange? Sue has shared how she feels, thinks, and believes. Instead of being heard, her thoughts are immediately attacked.

How might you deal differently with Sue? Your goal would be to understand Sue's position while at the same time maintain an open point of view about the situation.

Evaluating Your Communication

You will be given an opportunity to assess your ability to communicate in difficult situations. Respond naturally to the following statements in the blank spaces provided. At the end of this chapter you will again be given an opportunity to respond with the skills you have developed in this chapter. This will provide a chance for you to assess your progress in communication skills.

Respond To The Feeling

Imagine You Are A Parent

Situation 1.   Your son says, "It just isn't fair. My brother gets everything he wants and you won't buy me anything. Now you go out and buy him a bicycle. You like him more than you like me!"

Your response:

Situation 2. Your daughter says, "I hate you! Just because it's raining outside a little bit, you won't let me play in the yard with Doreen. And look at the fun she's having."

Your response:

Imagine You Are A Teacher

Situation 3. Your student says, "Up to this year I earned straight A grades. Now, since I have you, I'm getting B's. I can't understand it because I'm working just as hard as ever."

Your response:

Imagine You Are A Supervisor

Situation 4. A worker says, "As you can see, I'm working very hard, but the guy you put with me keeps slacking off and this gives me double work. We aren't going to get all of the work done."

Your response:

Is Anyone Listening?

Do you ever hear disconnected conversations such as the following one?

> *Mother:* "Johnny's teacher called today. She said he has really been acting up in school recently. And not only that, she said he's in danger of failing math!"
> *Father:* "Oh, is that so? Do you know where the newspaper is, honey? I wonder who's playing in the Monday night football game."
> *Mother:* "Will you please talk to your son about this matter?"
> *Daughter:* "Mom, can I tell Dad what I'm going to dress up like for Halloween?"
> *Johnny:* "Can I go out and play now? I finished all my meat."

Does this type of conversation sound familiar? Who is listening? The answer is—no one! No one is really listening to the serious concerns of each of the other family members. If this conversation were a piece of music, it certainly would not be a peaceful, smooth, harmonious composition with a unified theme. Each person is focused on his or her own interests and consequently four selfish themes are present. The mother is concerned about the possibility of her son failing math. The father's theme focuses on his needs. Their daughter is interested in talking about how she will dress for Halloween. Finally, Johnny, disinterested in any of the other three themes, just wants to go outside to play. The participants are engaged in what Tom Lenich calls a "Shoot and Reload dialogue" (Lenich, 1979). This occurs when one person in a conversation talks (shoots) while the other is busy thinking about what he or she is going to say next, instead of listening (reloads). How can any person possibly help any other person when this type of communication takes place?

Effective communication involves getting into the other person's world by attentive listening and then communicating to the person your understanding of that world through accurate responding. Accurate responding doesn't ignore the message but reflects clearly the feelings and meanings in the message. This attentive and accurate listening and responding removes the barriers that often hinder effective communication and rewarding relationships.

Selfish listening and responding hinder effective communication. In this type of communication, the communicator spends time judging rather than listening to the concerns of the other person. If you are going to encourage another person, you need to work continuously at understanding the meaning and feelings of the discouraged person and then communicate them back accurately.

A major problem in effective listening is the challenge involved in following closely what is being said. We often have a tendency to become distracted when other people are speaking. We are preparing what we are going to say next rather than attempting to understand their message and deal with their feelings and attitudes. How many people in your circle of relationships pay full attention to you when you talk? Do you more commonly feel people look in different directions, change the topic to something of interest to them, and fail to get your message? Have you had the experience of expressing personal accomplishment with real confidence and pride only to be told, "That's nothing. You should hear what happened to me."

When you are expressing your feelings and trying to say something important, often the listener is not focused on you. Be aware of what is going on when you are in the process of talking with others and what is happening with their listening behavior. You will become aware of the problems in truly listening to each other.

First, accurate listening shows you are involved and fully attentive. You have eye-to-eye contact. Your body posture is relaxed and shows you are involved (showing your presence). Second, accurate listening involves perceiving the speaker's messages (verbal and nonverbal) and understanding the speaker's theme.

Showing Your Presence In The Relationship

You show your presence when you create an atmosphere in which other people feel safe to discuss their concerns. You are present by providing time and by attending to their needs. You show an interest in what concerns them. You are making an unselfish commitment to hear them. Your physical presence involves eye-to-eye contact and a relaxed body posture.

Eye Contact

Effective listeners have the ability to use an ideal amount of eye-to-eye contact when communicating. What is ideal? Obviously, too little or no eye contact might convey disinterest. On the other hand, constant staring may be threatening and produce defensiveness in the speaker. The ideal amount is one with which you feel comfortable but with few breaks in contact. When you are truly listening, your body confirms that.

Another function of eye contact is to convey your empathy for the other person's concerns. Often, when we interrupt people while they are speaking, they lose their train of thought. By conveying through your eyes that you are in touch, you communicate your presence without distracting interruption.

Listening For The Speaker's Theme

Encouraging people show their presence in the relationship through eye contact and a natural, relaxed body posture which opens the door for further exploration of concerns. Encouragers need skills to better understand these concerns. Effective listening involves a thorough understanding of the theme of the speaker's message. This theme can be understood in a variety of ways. In this chapter, we discuss understanding the theme first through focusing on the speaker's words and feelings and, finally, through focusing on the speaker's body language.

Listening For The Words And Feelings

Encouragers listen attentively and nonjudgmentally to the words and feelings of the discouraged person. This is especially true in the early stages of a relationship. Unselfish listening involves resisting the tendency to focus on "how does this interest me" or "I'd rather talk about what I think your problem really is." Here are a few examples of selfish and judgmental listening:

> *Teacher:* "I taught a tremendous science lesson today. It was on molecules and the students were really turned on!"
>
> *Principal* (selfish listening): ""I remember the time I taught that lesson. She could really profit from my ideas."
>
> *Principal* (judgmental listening): "She said she had a good lesson. Huh, I'll bet there was chaos in the rooms."
>
> *Principal* (unselfish listening to the words and feelings): "Mrs. Jones seems to be feeling enthused about her lesson today. She'd probably like to tell me a lot more about her success story."

Listening to the theme involves staying on the topic the other person starts rather than introducing a new one. It also involves trying to look at the world through the other person's eyes.

Exercise 1. June, your six-year-old daughter, says, "I'm never going to school anymore. That teacher is always yelling at me in front of my friends."
What might June's theme be?

How might June be feeling?

Exercise 2. Joe, your student, says "Nobody wants to play with me at recess. I just know that it's because I'm so small. I can hear them laughing at me all of the time because of my size."
What might Joe's theme be?

What might Joe's feelings be?

Did you stay on the topic? Did you resist the temptation to judge or bring your own world into the problem? If so, you have heard the speaker. You have effectively listened.

Another way of improving listening skills will be discussed next. This is listening with your eyes to improving your sensitivity to the speaker's nonverbal clues.

Listening To Nonverbal Communication

People communicate in many ways. Encouragers are aware of the theme of the speaker's words and feelings as well as the theme of the speaker's nonverbal behaviors. Any information available to the encourager about the discouraged person is helpful in facilitating the encouragement process. Nonverbal clues are as important as words in understanding and helping people.

Sometimes nonverbal acts are consistent with verbal messages; for example, a person pounds the desk while expressing anger toward someone. However, sometimes nonverbal acts are incongruent with people's words; for example, someone tells you he or she agrees with you but sits in a closed, disagreeing position.

In the initial stages of relationship building, it is generally ineffective to confront the person with these inconsistencies. Confrontations, poorly timed, can produce defensiveness and discourage further exploration. However, it is important to be aware of these inconsistencies. There might be a time when they can be appropriately discussed in the relationship. This issue will be further addressed in the chapter on encouraging mutual feedback.

Application Of Listening To Nonverbal Cues

A few exercises are provided to further develop your ability to listen to the speaker's nonverbal cues.

Exercise 1. Observe the relationship between the verbal and nonverbal behaviors of people. Think how body language may reveal each of the following emotions or situations. Act out each one.

1. Pity me—look at how hard I have it.

2. You make me angry.

3. What a surprise!

4. Your actions shocked me.

5. Your behavior is annoying.

6. Things are bad, but maybe there is some hope.

7. Nobody cares about me.

8. I'm confused.

Group Exercise 1. Have each member of the group choose an emotion. Have a few people mime an emotion that is revealed in body language. Have the other members of the group guess what the person is feeling. Which emotions are the easiest to detect? Which are difficult to detect?

Group Exercise 2. Tell the other members of the group about a time when you tried to act in a way that you didn't really feel and someone sensed this inconsistency through your body language. How did you feel?

Group Exercise 3. Divide the participants into groups of three. Identify who will be person A, person B, and person C in each group. Person A speaks to person B about a time when he or she won something and gives the details of the occasion. Without speaking, person B shows his or her presence through eye contact. Person C observes how many eye contact breaks occurred during this one-minute exercise. Each person provides feedback to the other two people about what was happening.

Group Exercise 4.   Reverse roles until each participant has had a chance to speak, to listen, and to observe the eye contact of others.

References

Ivey, Allen E. *Microcounseling.* Springfield, IL: Chas. C. Thomas, 1971.

Ivey, Allen E. and N. Gluckstern. *Basic Attending Skills.* North Amherst, MA: Microtraining Associates, Inc., 1974.

Lenich, Tom. Personal conversation, 1979.

5 Responding With Understanding

When you respond with understanding, you respond in a way in which the other person feels truly understood.

Jack is the one everyone at work goes to when they have a problem. He's the one who listens closely, identifies what has been said, and then deals with the other person's concerns and perceptions. Unlike the type of conversation which occurs when you present a problem and the other person responds, "I've had it worse than that," Jack is interested in focusing on your concerns.

At home he is sensitive to his wife's concerns. His children, Beth in high school and Jerry in middle school, always come to him when they have something to talk about. They know he'll hear and understand them and they know he'll help them solve their problems.

Jack is approached at work by Dick. He wants to talk to Jack about a problem he is having making a sale with one of his regular customers. Dick indicates he is having some difficulty staying focused on the topic. As a result, he is not convincing in the sales talk he delivers.

Jack indicates, "You feel it is more difficult to talk with this customer." Dick indicates that's exactly how he is feeling. Jack says, "Tell me more about that." Dick continues, "Well, when I get there, I guess I am still dealing with the aftershocks of the contacts I have had earlier at home." Jack listens but nothing more is said. He says, "The problem you had at home is influencing your work." Dick starts to talk about the continuous arguments with his wife and the hostile environment at home.

In this brief vignette, you can see how responding with understanding and helping identify the real meaning of the problem helps people to feel understood and enables them to solve their own problems.

An effective response involves listening attentively and understanding the meaning of the message. Understanding what happens after a person talks and listening become crucial in the communication process. Many conversations between family members are almost totally disconnected. It's as if no one is on the other end of the line.

> *Mother:* "Billy's teacher called today. She says he has been misbehaving in school and he's now in danger of failing both math and English."
> *Father:* "Oh, do you know if the newspaper was delivered today? By the way, where did you put the mail?"
> *Mother:* "Please talk to your son about this situation."
> *Daughter:* "Mom, can I tell dad my ideas for the party we are going to have at our house next week?"

In this type of conversation, everyone talks but no one listens and no one communicates. If anyone has a serious concern, it is quickly bypassed for a personal interest. As a result, all you hear is a series of disconnected, personalized themes.

> Sue comes home distraught and crying. She says, "Jack told me he doesn't like me anymore and our relationship is over. I spent three years with him and I just can't believe he is dumping me."
> Her well-intentioned roommate says, "Oh, well, that's probably discouraging, but he's not the only boy in the neighborhood."

Imagine you are Sue. Feel her despair, discouragement, and upset feelings. It seems as if your world is coming apart. Now, imagine you have been told not to worry because there are many other boys available. How would you respond to this well-intentioned comment by someone who has not heard your feelings?

People can improve their ability to listen and respond in a more encouraging way. Encouraging teachers, sales personnel, supervisors, and even friends are often described as people who "listen and understand my feelings." Obviously, if the discouraged person isn't understood, understanding cannot possibly take place. Encouragement begins by understanding the way the discouraged person looks at life. Unless you begin with empathy and understanding, your response will be insensitive and ineffective.

Effective communication involves both understanding the other person's world (listening) and conveying your understanding to that person (responding). Barriers that hinder mutual understanding can be broken down through accurate listening and responding.

The biggest hindrance to effective communication is selfish listening and responding. The selfish communicator spends time judging rather than listening to the concerns of the other person. Encouragers work continuously to understand the meanings and feelings of the discouraged person.

The complex skill of communication can be divided into listening and responding. This chapter focuses on improving the first of these communication components—listening.

At first glance, listening appears to be quite simple, yet accurate listening rarely occurs. We have a tendency to become distracted when another person is speaking. We judge what is being said rather than listen for feelings.

How many people do you know who fully attend to you when you talk? More commonly, you may find that a person looks in different directions or switches the topic so you can't complete your message. How often do you hear someone express a personal accomplishment with pride, only to be followed by, "Oh, that's nothing! I've done better."

List a few pet annoyances (habits, attitudes, mannerisms) in yourself or others that you find interfere with effective communication.

Leaning how to listen effectively to feelings and beliefs is a major challenge. After you have become skilled in the listening process, you may wonder, "What do I say next?" In some instances, certain responses may discourage people.

Effective responses are essential not only in creating and accepting a nonthreatening atmosphere, but in helping people move in a direction at a pace with which they feel comfortable. As a listener, you will either add to or subtract from the courage, self-esteem, and confidence that are being developed in the person. The following example shows how three responses might steer the conversation in three different directions.

Experience ten-year-old Jerry's world and imagine how you would feel hearing these three different responses:

> *Jerry* (after receiving a D in math, which keeps him off the honors list): "I worked so hard on this math and I still didn't get the B I needed. I'm going to quit school."

> *Response 1:* "Quitting school is absurd. You are only ten and the state law requires you to be at least sixteen before you can quit. So you have six more years of school whether you like it or not!"

Given this response, how would you feel if you were Jerry?

What would you say if you were Jerry?

> *Response 2:* "Running away won't help. Face reality—you must study harder if you expect to do better!"

Given this response, how would you feel if you were Jerry?

How would you feel about this relationship if you were Jerry? What might you say next if you were Jerry?

> *Response 3:* "You sure sound discouraged. It's disappointing and a real let-down to work so hard to reach a goal and not make it."

Given this response, how would you feel if you were Jerry?

What might you say next if you were Jerry?

Did you find that your feeling and even the relationship would have traveled in different directions as a result of the three different responses? In what ways did they differ?

The third response was the one most likely to encourage further self-exploration. If you are going to encourage, you need to respond in ways that are unselfish and open, ways that convey understanding. You need to have social interest, the desire to cooperate and work with others. The encourager then becomes a unique and valuable factor in the growth and development of another person.

Response Styles That Discourage

People play a number of roles when they aren't sure about how to handle feeling that are being expressed by others. Some of these roles interfere with effective communication. Briefly, these roles include the following:

1. **Commanders-in-chief** order, command, and threaten to keep others in line. Relationships have more vertical than horizontal focus and are based primarily on power.

2. **Moralists** preach about the best way. They communicate by a lot of "shoulds," "oughts," and "musts" and often elicit shame, guilt, and doubt in others, which hinders and blocks communication.

3. **Judges** pronounce a person guilty without the need to evaluate, know/hear all the facts, weigh the evidence, or conduct a trial. All the answers in life are clear-cut, black or white. Judges are always certain they are right and you are wrong.

4. **Critics** ridicule, embarrass, and use sarcasm and thereby discourage people. They enjoy the position of being one up and seeing others one down.

5. **Psychologists** analyze, diagnose, and question, always believing they are able to explain the other person's intentions. When you are in contact with them, you tend to feel helpless and threatened which, of course, blocks communication.

Response Styles That Encourage

Responses determine the development of a relationship. When you use responses that dominate, moralize, or sympathize, you discourage the other person and you block self-exploration and increased awareness. The other person learns to respond by defending, attacking, giving up, or feeling worthless.

When you respond in a way that facilitates a relationship, the other person feels safer, more open, and less defensive and is more willing to talk about his or her concerns. After you know what those concerns are, you may be better able to encourage that person.

The most effective responses which lead to this exploration are those that focus on the other person, invite further exploration, and understand rather than judge.

Effective responses include the following.

Focusing On The Other Person

It is important to focus on what the other person believes or intends to communicate. Words may confuse or hide the meaning. Your focus is concentrated on the major goal of the message.

Have you ever said something that was taken in a totally different way than it was meant? Give an example in connection with your social relationships, family life, or work life.

To Develop Focusing On The Other Person:

- Stay on the topic presented.
- Attend closely to what is said.
- Recognize silence as part of the communication.
- When responding, use the word "you" or the person's name.
- Always focus on what the person is saying means to *them*, instead of how it affects *you*.
- Be a clear and accurate mirror. What is said is what you respond to.
- Don't react out of your interpretation or your needs.
- Listen. Don't conclude where the person is going before they get there.
- Be aware of how your response will be received.
- Invite exploration.

Stay on the other person's topic. Keeping focused on the topic requires considerable effort. You may need more information in order to acquire a better understanding of the feelings and beliefs that are being expressed. Questioning the person may produce defensiveness, create barriers or doubt, and indicate you are more interested in questioning than in understanding.

Certain approaches will help you gather more information without becoming a threat and without taking the lead. Ivey and Gluckstern (1974) have shown how the use of (1) open-ended questions and (2) "minimal encouragers" can show people you are "with them" while avoiding the trap of leading the communication.

Inviting Exploration

Inviting exploration through open-ended questions is another style of responding. While some questions are ineffective, the most productive questions are those that invite information rather than set up barriers. Ivey and Gluckstern (1974) wrote on the use of questions:

> The client comes into an interview with something that he/she feels is a problem. The initial task of the interviewer is to stay out of the interviewee's way so as to find out how the client sees his/her situation. Most useful in determining this is the technique of providing limited structure through the use of an open invitation to talk.
>
> *Open:* Could you tell me a little bit about your marriage? How do you feel about that?
>
> *Closed:* Are you married? Do you get along with your wife/husband?
>
> It may be observed that open comments provide room for the client to express his/her real self without the imposed categories of the interviewer. An open comment allows the client an opportunity to explore himself/herself with the support of the interviewer. A closed invitation to talk, on the other hand, often emphasizes factual content as opposed to feelings, demonstrates a lack of interest in what the client has to say, and frequently attacks or puts the client in his/her place. Closed questions can usually be answered in a few words or with a "yes" or "no."

Suppose that this is your first meeting with Jack (age 22). Consider the following comment and jot down a closed question. Follow your closed question with a possible response.

> *Jack:* "Well, I have this problem—you see, I lack confidence."

An example of a closed question is "How old are you?" Give some other examples of closed responses.

Now consider Jack's statement again and ask an open-ended question. For example, "Can you tell me more about it?"

How might Jack respond to the open-ended question?

What are some other open-ended questions you might ask?

Feelings And Theme

Understanding the feelings and theme is the most important element in effective communication. Adler referred to understanding as far back as 1924. He called this understanding or social interest empathy. Adler defined empathy as "the ability to see with the other's eyes and hear with the other's ears and feel with the other's heart."

What does empathic understanding involve? First, it means non-evaluative listening and withholding judgment of the other person's message. Judgments become barriers to completed messages. Carl Rogers (1961) suggested:

...the major barrier to mutual interpersonal communication is our very natural tendency to judge, evaluate, to approve or disapprove, the statements of the other person or group...Although the tendency to make evaluations is common in almost all interchange of language, it is very much heightened in those situations where feelings and emotions are deeply involved.

But is there any way of solving this problem, of avoiding this barrier? Real communication occurs, and the tendency to evaluate is avoided, when we listen with understanding. What does this mean? It means seeing the idea and attitude expressed from the other person's point of view, sensing how it feels to him or her, achieving his or her frame of reference in regard to what he or she is talking about.

Communications Rating Scale

This scale is designed to rate effective versus ineffective responses. It is just a guideline and should not be used as an absolute.

1.0 Level Responses
A. Responses that focus on self rather than on the other person
B. Responses that take the subject off the topic
C. Responses that tend to discourage, dominate, or moralize
D. Responses that lack feelings and theme
E. Questions that could produce defensiveness

2.0 Level Responses
A. Responses that partially pick up the theme but show no understanding of feelings
B. Responses that partially pick up the feelings but show no understanding of the theme
C. Open questions and minimal encouragement

3.0 Level Responses
A. Responses that are other-person centered

B. Responses that stay on the topic and show both feelings and theme

Additional Suggestions For Improving Your Communication Skills

Ask yourself the following questions about what you say:

1. How does what I said fit in with what the other person said?

2. How does it relate to how the other person sees the world?

3. Is it of any interest to the other person?

4. At what level have I responded to the other person's level?

5. How did what I said show the other person that he or she contributed to what I said?

6. How did what I said contribute to continuing rather than ending the conversation?

7. What does what I said mean about you and me?

8. How honest is what I said?

9. In what possible ways might what I said be interpreted?

10. Did I discourage the other person by what I said?

11. How did I demonstrate that I listened to the other person?

12. Have I physically demonstrated that I listened to the other person?

13. How did I sound? Was I enthusiastic?

14. Was the other person more encouraged or more discouraged by what I said?

Application Of Responding With Understanding

Understanding through clear and accurate listening is basic to communication. What barriers to listening do you use that you are aware of? What keeps you from communicating so that the listener receives the meaning you intend to send?

The encouraged listener begins by identifying discouraging feeling and beliefs. What are some discouraging beliefs and feelings you have heard?

What are some communication styles you personally find discouraging?

What are some skills and attitudes you can develop to respond more openly and more effectively to the other person?

References

Adler, Alfred. *The Social Interest*. New York: Putnam, 1939.

Ivey, Allen E. and N. Gluckstern. *Basic Attending Skills*. North Amherst, MA: Microtraining Associates, Inc., 1974.

Rogers, Carl. *On Becoming a Person*. Boston, MA: Houghton-Mifflin, 1961.

6

Building Agreement Skills To Create A Bond

P eople tend to like people who they think are similar to themselves. It makes sense. If you and I meet in Australia and find that we both are from the United States, then Pennsylvania, and then Reading, Pennsylvania, we have an immediate connection. We will also start to subconsciously conclude a whole host of things about each other. We both probably like the Philadelphia Phillies, love soft pretzels with mustard, etc.

Joy immediately connects with everyone she meets. In a short period of time, you feel like you have known her for years. Joy quickly zeroes in on things she has in common with people and can turn areas of disagreement into agreements. When you are throwing a party, you want to make sure Joy is there so the party will be a success. She has an easy way of finding similarities between herself and others. Joy would be excellent in any profession that directly involves people, from selling to teaching to management.

Joy is a positive person who has agreement skills which help her to build bonds with people. Soon you will have the six agreement skills discussed in this chapter.

Positive people have the skills to instantly connect with others in a way that subtly communicates, "We are alike." By the end of a party, the positive person has circulated throughout the room, met everyone, and has everyone feeling that they have known this person for years. These skills of connecting with others are called *agreement skills.*

Agreement skills can be demonstrated in a variety of ways. In this chapter, we will discuss the types of agreement skills: (1) listening for similarities between you and the other person; (2) finding areas of agreement, even in disagreements; (3) getting people into a "yes" mood; (4) making "we" references; (5) starting with "and" instead of "but" when responding with a difference of opinion; and (6) employing similar body language, facial gestures, and pace of speech.

1. Listening For Similarities

Immediately upon meeting someone, the positive person is scanning for ways to connect by finding similarities. Three sources of similarities include common interests, common struggles, and common strengths and weaknesses.

Common Interests

> *Charlie (ninth grader):* "I'm really frustrated. I would like to play in the school band but my father won't let me. He thinks I should play football just because he did. Well, its not my thing. Music is."
>
> *Mr. Miller (counselor):* "You sure wish your father could understand that what he likes isn't necessarily what you like."
>
> *Charlie:* "Yeah."
>
> *Mr. Miller:* "Tell me, what instrument do you play?"
>
> *Charlie:* "The clarinet and a little bit of saxophone."
>
> *Mr. Miller:* "Wow, I love music! I never learned to play any instrument but I sure love to listen to music. Could you bring in your clarinet some day and play something?"
>
> *Charlie:* "Sure."
>
> *Mr. Miller:* "What is your favorite song to play?"
>
> *Charlie:* "I have lots of favorites. What's yours?"

Mr. Miller's interest in music helped Charlie to re-energize his interest. Charlie thinks that maybe his liking music is okay. After all, if Mr. Miller, whom he respects, has a similar interest, he himself can't be that strange. Whether or not his father allows Charlie to pursue his love of music, Charlie knows that he can drop his mask in front of at least one adult.

Common Struggles

> *Al (high school student):* "I applied to six colleges that I really wanted to go to and was turned down by each."
>
> *Uncle John:* "That's really frustrating for you, huh!" (empathy)
>
> *Al:* "Sure is. I don't know what I'm going to do with myself."
>
> *Uncle John:* "You know, Al, I really wanted to be a pilot at one time but my vision kept me out. I dreamt, slept, and constantly thought about it, and when the rejection hit me it was like a brick wall."
>
> *Al:* "What did you do?"
>
> *Uncle John:* "I kept trying to find something similar, at least where good vision was not a requirement."
>
> *Al:* "Maybe I can apply to a few other colleges and if I still don't succeed, find out what else I can do."

Al found out that his uncle was just like him in a way. He, too, experienced rejection in his lifetime and wasn't devastated by it. He demonstrated to Al that there was still hope and many alternatives. He didn't tell Al what to do, but through his experience he helped Al see that he doesn't have to be perfect to be accepted by his uncle. Perhaps Al previously didn't want to let his uncle down by admitting the rejections. Now he was free of that burden.

Common Strengths And Weaknesses

Helping people to develop the "courage to be imperfect" has been stressed continually throughout this book. The willingness to be imperfect opens a whole world of possibilities for people. It is a paradox to attempt to talk about the courage to be imperfect while being the perfect model, similar to the following dialogue between a doctor and a patient who was in complete traction:

> *Patient:* "How am I doing, Doc? Will I walk soon?"
> *Doctor:* "Oh, I wouldn't worry about it if I were you."
> *Patient:* "No, and I wouldn't worry about it if I were you either."

It is easy for the encourager to talk about the courage to be imperfect, but being imperfect is difficult. By focusing on common weaknesses or imperfections, the encourager points out his or her own humanness. To the discouraged person, the message is, "He or she lives these beliefs; therefore, so can I."

Discouraged people frequently criticize themselves and have difficulty accepting encouragement of their assets and strengths. By nonapologetically showing a similarity between a strength that both the discouraged person and the encourager have, the encourager makes it okay to talk about positive points.

Think of other areas besides interests, struggles, and strengths and weaknesses in which to do similarity focusing.

2. Finding Areas Of Agreement, Even In Disagreement

In addition to listening for similarities or commonalties between yourself and another, another agreement skill is to find areas of agreement, even when disagreeing about an issue. The idea that opposites attract, while possibly true in the physical sciences, is quite false in the science of human relations. While long-lasting relationships have some differences on the surface ("She's outgoing, I'm quiet"), at a deeper level they are quite similar ("We both believe in God").

The positive person is constantly listening with an ear toward finding areas in which all sides agree. This is especially facilitative during strong disagreements. Sense Betty's use of an agreement skill by focusing on an area where she agrees with Joan:

> *Joan:* "You think that the government should care for the needy, and I think that creates a dependency on the government."
>
> *Betty:* "Then we both agree that things as they are today just aren't working, don't we?"
>
> *Joan:* "Absolutely."

Agreement skills can also be used in a rather curious and creative way when dealing with a hostile person's direct attack. Take some time to sense Bill's use of agreement skills with Ed:

> *Ed:* "I think you are a real phony."
>
> *Bill:* "I agree."
>
> *Ed:* "What! You agree that you're a phony?"
>
> *Bill:* "I agree that *you think* I'm a phony. We are in agreement. We both agree that *you think* I'm a phony. And I think it is only fair that if I agree that *you think* I'm a phony, then you will agree that *I don't think* I'm a phony!"

A positive person can comfortably agree with a person who disagrees with him or her. In other words, when in a disagreement with someone, practice reflecting what the other person is saying and adding that you agree that is the way the other person feels.

3. Getting People Into A "Yes" Mood

The positive person orchestrates an upbeat rhythm in all relationships, skillfully avoiding unnecessary noise in conversations. This is done by talking about the other person's interests and by asking questions such that they are likely to elicit "yes" answers.

"No" is negative, isn't it? Yes! Throughout our life, when we hear or see or say the word no, we accumulate tens of thousands of negative associations. The positive person doesn't want to be linked with negative associations and carefully rephrases questions in his or her mind to bring out a "yes" response.

> *Negative salesperson:* "You don't want a shirt with your new suit, do you?"
>
> *Customer:* "Uh, no."

> *Positive salesperson:* "Did you say your name is Charlie?" ("yes" question)
> *Customer:* "Yes."
>
> *Salesperson:* "This suit looks great on you. Does it feel great?"
> *Customer:* "Yes"
>
> *Salesperson:* "Would you like to look at a shirt and tie to complement your new suit?"
> *Customer:* "Yes, I'd love to."

Practice phrasing questions to generate "yes" responses in others.

4. Making "We" References

To reinforce similarity and agreement, the positive person invites the other person under his or her umbrella by using "we," "our," and "us" statements.

> *Elaine:* "I hate rain!"
> *Rachel:* "People like us prefer sunshine, don't we?" ("we" reference)
> *Elaine:* "Yes, we sure do."

5. Starting With "And" Instead Of "But"

When one person makes a point and the other person responds with "but…," the first person tends to tighten, clench fists, back up, get defensive, and prepare for his or her own re**but**tal. The positive person knows that even when in disagreement, it is more effective to start with the word "and" instead. "And" keeps both parties in an agreement mood, and thus the other person will tend to listen rather than judge.

Using "and" when in disagreement takes much practice but offers rich rewards. Practice by really listening to yourself say the word "but" and rephrasing it with a big smile on your face, your head nodding in agreement, and starting your response with an "and."

6. Employing Similar Body Language, Facial Gestures, And Pace Of Speech

When people are in tune with each other, they will slowly gravitate to subconsciously imitate each other's mannerisms, gestures, expressions, and speech. The positive person does this consciously.

Remember the following ideas to slowly get in sync with others:

1. The more you sit or use your arms in a manner similar to the other person, the more the other person will feel in agreement with you.

2. The more your facial gestures are in sync with the other person, the more the other person feels in agreement with you.

3. The faster or slower the other person speaks, the faster or slower you speak, and the other person will feel in agreement with you.

Agreement Skills Make Connections And Build Bonds For Positive People

Positive people realize that they can have a greater impact on people when they are in agreement. Getting people into an agreement mood has the advantage of building trust and believability and communicating a sense of synchronicity. Using agreement skills also eliminates the detouring influence of disagreements between people.

Application Of Agreement Skills

1. Whenever meeting someone new, immediately connect with the other person by finding at least three things in common.

2. Think of someone with whom you currently disagree on an issue. Identify at least three areas in which you do agree.

3. Imagine hearing someone with whom you totally disagree presenting their side of a story. After listening to what the other person might say, practice responding by starting with the word "and" instead of "but" while nodding your head.

4. Make "we" references to the following statements:

    A. "I think that people should treat each other with respect." *Your response* (e.g., "We..." or "People like us agree that..." or "You and I both..."):

    B. "You shouldn't have to take a foreign language in school if you are never going to use it." *Your response:*

    C. "I love the Dallas Cowboys!" *Your response:*

7

Believing Skills To Communicate Your Respect

Don believes in you—even more than you believe in yourself. Don is constantly communicating to you that you are the kind of person who "can do it." He encourages you to set high standards, achieve big goals, take risks, and go after your dream. Don sees something unique and special in you. When you are with him, you are creative and more certain of yourself. You want to prove to Don that you can do it, but it seems that Don already knows that, and he is more interested in you proving it to yourself. Don would make a great manager or any type of leader, from a coach to a teacher.

Don has believing or respecting skills. In this chapter, you will focus on developing your skills to believe in yourself and others.

A positive person knows that a prerequisite for being able to genuinely encourage others is confidence and respect. Your confidence is a product of having self-esteem or a sense of personal effectiveness—a belief that you are a capable person who is able to function and meet life's challenges. In certain ways, we live in a confusing culture which conveys the message that if you think less of yourself, feel inadequate, and are overly humble, you are alright. However, if you have self-esteem, self-respect, and self-confidence, you are suspected of having something wrong with you, being less than humble, or perhaps even neurotic.

The positive, mentally healthy person feels good about himself or herself and is able to assess personal assets, strengths, and resources instead of only limitations; furthermore, he or she owns, recognizes, and values those assets.

Confidence is built as an individual is encouraged to be more *independent* and *responsible*. Insofar as an individual is kept dependent upon others, he or she feels inept and discouraged, with reduced self-esteem. When we encourage independence, we convey "you can do it." Responsibility is freely given instead of earned.

How might you communicate respect and confidence in the following situations?

1. Your child is doing his math homework. He has a tendency to give up quickly. He looks at his homework and says, "I just can't get these problems. They are too hard."
   What do you say? What do you do?

2. Your teenager comes home discouraged and dejected. She lost her boyfriend two weeks ago and says, "It's Thursday and I don't have a date for Saturday's dance. It's embarrassing. I wish I were dead."
   What do you say? What do you do?

3. Your husband comes home from work looking despondent. He has been a top salesman for his company and just lost his major client. He says, "Now we are really in trouble. I can't meet the mortgage and all these bills with less income."
   What do you say? What do you do?

4. A friend who started tennis lessons four months ago has just lost in the second round of the club tournament, 6-0, 6-0. She is embarrassed and humiliated. She says, "I knew I shouldn't have taken up

tennis. I've never been coordinated and I just looked dumb out there."

What do you say? What do you do?

These are typical situations that test your desire to encourage. When we see people who are dejected losing confidence, we want to help.

Confidence and self-esteem are as essential to an effective mental approach to life as food and water are to physical survival and stability. That is an important concept to comprehend. We all recognize that we could not live for long without water and food. What we do not recognize is the deprivation and lack of psychological growth we experience when we do not nurture our confidence and self-esteem. If we are hungry, we look for something to eat; if we are thirsty, we find something to drink. However, when we lack self-confidence and self-esteem, we don't seem to know where to go to find them. Often, we act as if we don't have confidence and self-esteem, as if we are without them and there is no way to obtain them. We are living in the prison of hopelessness—and our sentence appears to be for life!

Self-confidence comes from your personal reservoir of past successes in mental, physical, occupational, social, emotional, or other areas. Something you are very capable of doing may provide you with the necessary self-confidence. As you behave effectively (for example, solving a problem, performing a physical skill, or in your relations with others), you increase your self-confidence.

Self-confidence also emerges from your ability to identify and enumerate your resources. As you become sensitive to your vast potential to behave in ways which result in confidence, you will be impressed with the power within your grasp.

Stop for a moment to think about some of your personality strengths. For example, being sensitive, understanding, or courageous can all be personality strengths. In the same way, being a good listener or a caring and concerned person are strengths. Complete the following strength acknowledgment exercise, first for yourself and later for others. List six of your strengths; these are the resources you have which stimulate self-confidence.

1.

2.

3.

4.

5.

6.

Remember, we are more prepared to list our weaknesses, or liabilities, than our strengths. Perhaps you were unable to develop an adequate list of resources or strengths. If you made a full effort but were unsuccessful, you might check with someone who knows you well and who is empathic; ask him or her to add to your list. Either way, encourage yourself to ask someone for feedback about yourself.

It is very important to establish your own self-confidence if you are going to be able to communicate it to others.

Confidence also plays a role for people in business and sales. People who really believe in their product instead of viewing it as just a means for personal gain exude a confidence which is contagious. They become financially successful too.

Fred is a minister in a suburban area where people are concerned with getting ahead, competing, winning, and being first. He is a confident, concerned person who is involved with the young as well as the aged. He communicates respect and confidence. People feel better about themselves after their contact with Fred. His ministry supports, heals, values, and encourages. Why is Fred so effective? Why may other ministers be much less effective?

You communicate confidence to another person by showing your belief in that person, which stimulates his or her confidence. Communicating this belief involves being perceptive and sincere. Confidence is not communicated by false bravado. Try to communicate confidence in the following scenarios.

Your son is entered in a tennis tournament and has reached the semi-finals. He is to play the top player in the tournament next. The night before the match, you can tell he is discouraged. He says, "It's hopeless. I might as well forfeit. Bill is far too quick and strong for me."

Your response:

Your wife is scheduled to give a major presentation. There will be many important, intelligent people in the audience. Before leaving, she says to you, "I'm really scared. Many of the people in the audience know more about the topic than I do."

Your response:

Your husband has the difficult task of having to let a long-time employee of his company know that her services are no longer needed. He feels guilty and inept. He really doesn't support the policy and feels the employee is being treated unfairly. He says, "I don't know how I can go ahead and fire her."

Your response:

If you are a communicator who does not communicate confidence, you probably even communicate your lack of confidence. For example,

> To your son, the tennis player, you might say, "Don't worry. You're still the best player in our family."

> To your wife, who is scheduled to make a major presentation, you might say, "I still think you're great, so stop being concerned."

> To your husband, who has to fire an employee, you might say, "You never did have the courage to do what is expected of you."

A more appropriate response in each of these situations might be:

> To your son, who indicates it is hopeless, say, "Knowing you, I'm sure you'll do fine. Play as well as you can and you'll learn a lot."

> To your wife, who is scheduled to make a major presentation, say, "You feel unsure of yourself, but I have heard you talk and I'm sure you will do fine."

> To your husband, who has to fire an employee, say, "You're feeling conflict. You are asked to do something you don't believe in. You are very honest and sincere, and I'm sure this will be communicated to her."

Encouragement requires that you develop a special language, a language that communicates confidence. If you are to communicate confidence, you can do it best by reaching into the reservoir of your own positive feelings about yourself and your belief in people's potential to move confidently toward challenges.

What do you see when you look at a glass that is half full of water? Some people see the full part and say it is half full; others see the empty part and say it is half empty.

When you communicate confidence, you will be able to see and value the half-full glass. This means that you will be able to focus on a person's positive traits—patience, perseverance, energy, steadfastness, concern—and communicate your recognition of these traits.

Think of some people you have regular contact with (parents, spouse, children, employer, employees, clients, colleagues, neighbors, customers, friends). Identify two traits they have which make you feel confident in them.

Now, how will you communicate your confidence? You might begin by stating, "I have confidence in your judgment, enthusiasm, and ability." You could continue by taking a trait or ability they have and enlarging on it. As you value this trait, the person comes to feel more confident. Think about how you could show confidence in the following situations:

> Your young child has just dropped and broken a plate.

Your spouse has pulled off the highway and caused an accident.

Your secretary has mailed a letter that you had not completed.

One of your sales staff has just lost a big sale.

Respect comes from believing that all people are equal as human beings and have the right to be treated equally. This means that although they may vary in age, ability, wealth, or other traits, they deserve the dignity of equal treatment.

When you have respect, you show faith in another's worth and potential. You value and are committed to that person's growth. Since most self-respect is often a reflection of the support and sense of value we get from others, this respect increases the individual's self-respect and self-confidence.

What are some ways in which you show respect to others regardless of their situation?

What are some ways in which you are now aware that you show lack of respect because you do not treat people as equals?

Respect and confidence are essential for communicating encouragement. However, because of self-interest and competitiveness, we often neglect their importance. They are attitudinal outgrowths of what we believe about ourselves and people in general.

Application Of Believing Skills

1. What would you like to do in your lifetime but feel you can't? Communicate respect in your abilities. Imagine what you could tell yourself to encourage yourself to go for it. (For

example, focus on what's right with you, previous achievements, moments of courage, etc.)

2. Think of someone in your life who is anxious about a change he or she is going to experience. How can you encourage the other person to build their confidence about the change?

8

Enthusiasm Skills To Create Energy

Gabrielle loves life and enjoys every moment of it. She is full of energy and exudes enthusiasm about other people's interests and achievements. When she looks at pictures of someone's baby, Gabrielle seems as excited as the parent, while others just page through the photos with token comments. Gabrielle combines believing skills ("You can do it!") with enthusiasm skills ("Can you feel the excitement of graduation day in only one year?") to give a potential dropout the encouragement to hang in there. She would be a dynamite, turbo-charged salesperson or motivational speaker.

Gabrielle has enthusiasm skills. In this chapter, you will find yourself getting enthused about life's inspirational possibilities for yourself and others.

The positive person's most obvious characteristic is enthusiasm. Positive people are enthused about life and its unlimited possibilities. Positive people are also enthused about the potential in others. And positive people's enthusiasm adds value to everything they focus on.

Enthusiasm starts with enthusiasm about oneself.

Developing Your Positive Self-Image Through Enthusiasm

If you were to think of some of the characteristics of the best teacher you ever had, there is a good chance you would say that, first and foremost, this person was enthusiastic. If you think of the most encouraging person you ever met, you probably would say, among other characteristics, that this person was enthusiastic. Even when reflecting on the most interesting person you ever met, you might remember an aura of enthusiasm around him or her. Enthusiasm, a heightened energy level and an optimistic zest for life, is a characteristic developed by successful people. In fact, it is quite difficult to find extremely successful people who have not developed their self-image by developing their enthusiasm.

Enthusiasts are people who change the world. You, too, when fully fired up with enthusiasm, have a positive impact on yourself, other people, and life itself. Every time you create a smile on someone's face, you have just changed the world! When you are enthusiastic, you are more appealing, more popular, more influential, and even more attractive. Watch two people, one of whom is physically attractive but has a dullness of face and eyes and the other who perhaps is not as physically attractive but who has an enthusiastic facial expression, a warm smile, bright eyes, and a sense of aliveness. With whom would you prefer to associate? Yes, enthusiasm makes you more attractive. The enthusiast literally lights up a roomful of people just by opening the door. The enthusiast gives hope to the hopeless and energy to the dull.

It's no wonder that people who have a positive self-image are usually seen as being enthusiastic. It was originally thought that positive self-image produces enthusiasm, but the opposite is just as true. The simple fact is that not only does a positive self-image produce enthusiasm, but enthusiasm produces a positive self-image. That's right. If you follow closely these ideas in developing your enthusiasm, you can literally create a more positive self-image. Like a little snowball rolling down a snow-covered mountain and gathering more mass, your enthusiasm gathers more enthusiasm. And off you go on your winning streak.

Develop your positive self-image by igniting your never-failing powers of enthusiasm. Brace yourself and develop your enthusiasm by working on three different levels: (1) getting enthused about yourself, (2) getting enthused about other people, and (3) getting enthused about life.

Getting Enthused About Yourself, Your Uniqueness, And Your Talents

You are literally a miracle! You are such a rare combination of the physical and spiritual that there is no one, anywhere in the world, exactly like you. You are so special that you have been given the greatest gift in the world—you were selected to be a human being. You are the owner of your body, your mind, your actions, your thoughts, and your feelings. Even your dreams are uniquely yours. And this is your moment in the history of the magnificent universe. You are alive, which gives you the power to draw up the blueprint for the kind of person you want to be.

Tap those human powers that you have by igniting the power of enthusiasm for yourself and your possibilities. In fact, you are your possibilities in the beginning stages, waiting to happen. Your success happens when you turn on your electrical power of enthusiasm. But how do you turn on that electricity? How do you become enthusiastic? Simple. To become enthusiastic, all you have to do is **become enthusiastic!** That may sound simplistic, but it's true. You become enthusiastic by becoming enthusiastic. Watch how simple it is to develop a positive self-image by **becoming enthusiastic**.

1. Smile enthusiastically.   Wherever you go, watch the life-giving power that your smile has on people. We have asked thousands of people the question, "Who would you rather be with, an enthusiastic person or a person with a frown?" Does it surprise you to discover that not one single person preferred a frowning person? Be the energy wherever you go. Even if at first it seems unnatural to extend a warm welcome smile to everyone, it will soon be as natural to you as tying your shoes.

To realize the power of a smile, let's consider two people. We'll call the first person, who never smiles, I.M. Dull. How do you feel around I.M. Dull? I.M. Dull isn't very rewarding to be around. Would you buy anything from I.M. Dull? Would you enjoy listening to a lecture given by I.M. Dull? Probably not. Now consider the other person, a good listener, who meets you with a warm smile. Let's call this person N. Thusiastic. Isn't N. Thusiastic a more refreshing person to be around? Doesn't this person give you more life than I.M. Dull? No wonder people with a smile have a more positive self-image.

Remember, a smile creates a positive self-image. Get enthused about yourself. Become determined that you will light up the faces of people by your smile; then watch your self-image climb like a spaceship ascending from the launching pad at Cape Kennedy.

2. Walk enthusiastically.   Enthusiasts walk faster. They should— they are going places. Compare the walks of I.M. Dull and N. Thusiastic. While I.M. Dull walks with head down, shoulders curved inward, and a short apologetic step, N. Thusiastic walks with head up (even in the rain), shoulders back, and a crisp gait. Without meeting these two individuals, you draw conclusions about them just by observing their walks. Their walks tell a story.

Interestingly, research demonstrates that most victims of muggings tend to have a certain walk. Prisoners who were serving time for muggings agreed that a person's walk strongly influenced their decision to attack. The person most likely to become a mugging victim is one taking short, shuffling steps with the chest buried between the shoulders.

Remember, your walk stems from your self-image, but your self-image also stems from how you walk. Change the way you walk. Walk like an enthusiast and soon a positive self-image will become part of you. Win people over, even before you meet them, by your confident, enthusiastic walk.

3. Get psyched on yourself by speaking enthusiastically.   Modulate your voice. Every person can remember a never-ending speech given by a monotonous speaker. Yet the same words brought to life by an enthusiastic speaker can give energy to the group and make the talk more powerful. You can probably also remember teachers who gave no excitement to their lessons. Or perhaps you experienced a salesperson who described a house, a car, or a living room set with no life. The enthusiast puts vitality into the talk.

Hold people's attention by putting refreshment into everything you say. Say "hello" with life. Say "congratulations" with vigor. Say "have a great day" with meaning and genuine enthusiasm. When you "vitalize" things, something interesting happens. You actually invigorate yourself. When someone asks you how you are doing, do you just say "okay" or "not so good"? Enliven your response and watch how you can change your "okay" or "not so good" to "terrific!" or "fantastic!" You actually do become terrific or fantastic just by saying and feeling it.

4. Use a vocabulary filled with enthusiastic words.   More and more psychological research demonstrates the power of words on a person's emotions. If you think of it, depressed people tend to have a vocabulary filled with gloomy, inactive, depressing words. Contrarily, enthusiasts tend to have vocabularies overflowing with positive, active, assertive, enlivening words.

Two prominent behavioral scientists, Albert Ellis (co-author of *A New Guide to Rational Living*) and Charles Zastrow (author of *Talk to Yourself*) show how we create our emotions simply by the words we use. Change your life and your self-image by changing your vocabulary. Compare the vocabularies of our friends I.M. Dull and N. Thusiastic.

Failure vs. Success Vocabulary

I.M. Dull Says:	but	N. Thusiastic says:
"Things are awful, terrible."		"We face an exciting challenge."
"I hate aging"		"I love aging. After all, what is the alternative?"
"I'm way too old to change."		"My experiences give me an advantage in changing."
"Maybe it can be done."		"It absolutely can be done. I know the way to make it work."

"Things are okay."	"Things are great."
"Let's give up. It's no use."	"Okay, let's put ourselves into second gear."
"Good job."	"Fantastic performance."
"There are no answers."	"We have plenty of alternatives. Let's look for the best one."
"I've tried calling on that account before. They are too stubborn. Don't waste your time."	"I found one approach that didn't work on that account. Let's brainstorm and think about what the account needs and win it over."

Like the enthusiast, build your self-image on a foundation of strong, positive words. If you do, your emotions will change before your eyes. With a positive vocabulary and positive emotions, you become a powerful magnet, attracting positive people and success.

5. Wake up enthusiastically.   In the morning, when most people treat their alarm clocks like the enemy, look at your alarm clock as though it were a friendly fire alarm. When it rings, jump out of bed fired up with your enthusiasm. Put a glow in your mind and your heart. An enthusiastic start to the day gives you an advantage over the ho-hum person who needs an hour and a morning cup of coffee or a morning smoke to get going. Let your fire alarm ignite action and enthusiasm for the day. Remember, the way to become enthusiastic is simply to **become enthusiastic**.

6. Answer your phone enthusiastically.   Get off automatic pilot and get enthused every time the phone rings. Remember, the person calling is someone who has taken the time to phone you. Let the person catch your enthusiasm right from the start. While the programmed robot says a dull "Hello," the enthusiast answers with a cheery "Good afternoon" or "Top of the morning to you," or even "With a little good news for you, this could be both of our days." Develop new enthusiastic ways of answering the phone every day by letting your creativity flow. Your opening words on the phone are limited only by your creativity.

7. Listen enthusiastically. Win people over by employing the rarely used skill of enthusiastic listening. As you listen to people talk, lean forward. Use open, expressive eyes, conveying full attentiveness to the speaker's ideas. The world's best salespeople are not only great, enlivening speakers with positive vocabularies but enthusiastic listeners as well. Stay away from playing games like "Can you top this?" or "That reminds me of my experience. Let me tell you about it." Stay on the speaker's topic and watch your popularity soar!

8. Build your self-image by constantly analyzing your assets. While most people are more talented at seeing what is wrong rather than right with themselves, you should find only what's right with yourself. If you have positive points and you don't recognize them, you are lying to yourself. Don't lie to yourself and the world. The world needs you to be a success, and to be a success, you have to focus on your strengths. Relax, sit back for a few minutes, and think about the following questions:

- What have you accomplished that has given you real personal satisfaction? Include mental, parental, academic, social, physical, professional, financial, athletic, and spiritual accomplishments.

- What do you consider to be your five most positive assets? (Don't move on until you find at least five.)

- Think of the people you respect the most. What do you have in common with them? What do you have that they don't?

- Think of some things you have done for other people that were really helpful to them during difficult times in their lives. Think about a time when you helped someone to succeed with your encouragement.

- What can you give in a personal relationship?

- To whom could you really give a boost by making a surprise phone call? What characteristic do you have that could give this person a boost?

- Did you ever really want to achieve something and, after working hard for it, finally succeed? Recall the experience and jot down all of the positive traits that were necessary for you to succeed.

- Do you remember a time when you failed at something and, instead of giving up, came back stronger to overcome the failure? Relive the experience.

- Recall a time when enthusiasm made the difference for you either in your personal or professional life. What happened? How did it feel?

- What trait would you like to develop today? Combine your enthusiasm, your creative thinking, and your positive self-image, and "go for it."

Remember, a positive self-image is won by developing your enthusiasm. You become enthusiastic by **becoming enthusiastic**. Get enthused about yourself by smiling enthusiastically, walking enthusiastically, speaking enthusiastically, building a vocabulary of enthusiasm, walking up and answering your phone enthusiastically, listening enthusiastically, and analyzing your assets every single day. When you do this, you are on your road to Success City via the Enthusiastic Expressway.

Now that you have become enthused about yourself, focus your attention on ways to get enthused about other people.

Getting Enthused About Other People

Light the fires under everyone you meet with your enthusiasm. Pass on your positive energies and be a "pick 'em up" type of person. Be easy to talk to and give people a warm feeling when they are with you. In a world that has too much loneliness and lack of caring, you can become a natural source of warmth, encouragement, and enthusiasm. Enthusiasm makes the difference in your relationships with people.

How powerful is your enthusiasm in the lives of other people?

Consider the following illustration of how the power of enthusiasm works. Imagine that while you are out shopping, you cross paths with some friends. During your conversation with them, they casually invite you to a party they are having at their house the next day. Perhaps you wonder whether they are sincere about the invitation. You wonder why they did not invite you earlier if it was so important that you be there. You really do want to go. All day you struggle with the decision whether or not to go. The next day arrives, and bright and early that morning the telephone rings. Lo and behold, it's your friends, and they again extend their invitation, enthusiastically saying, "We are really looking forward to seeing you tonight. We have so many things to talk about. Please try to come."

The extra effort on your friends' part may have enhanced the possibility that you would go to their party. Like this second effort, genuine enthusiasm is the skill of extending additional energies or heightened invitations to others.

1. Get enthused about other people's lives. Be a stimulant instead of a depressant. Get excited about people's lives and work. Observe the different ways that I.M. Dull and N. Thusiastic listen to people.

Are You a Depressant or a Stimulant to People?

I.M. Dull says:	but	N. Thusiastic says:
"You say you're writing a book? I understand that it is almost impossible to get a publisher nowadays. I had a cousin who was the top student in her economics class at Harvard, and she wrote a book and couldn't find a single publisher. All that work and nothing out of it. I personally don't think that writing a book is worth the effort."		"You're writing a book? Wow, an author! I'll bet you're having a great time putting it together. You probably dream about it even in your sleep. And imagine the day that it comes out on the market and there's your name on the cover. Would you tell me a little about your ideas?"
"You're a hairdresser? I often wondered about you people. I would		"You're a hairdresser? Fantastic. It must be exciting to be in a pro-

think that your job would get quite boring; one customer after another all day, just standing there cutting hair."

fession where you help people to feel beautiful. You know, I've known people who wouldn't be seen out in public until they saw their stylist. You folks really do make a difference in people's lives. As I think of it, why not? After all, people come to you for more than just a styling. They come to you for courage, confidence, and hope. It must feel good being in such a rewarding profession."

Get enthused about people's lives and work. Be a stimulant and give them some of your energies. Get enthused about people. Be the rare stimulant who sees what's right with people and not what's wrong with them.

2. Work at remembering every person's name and a few important facts about him or her.   Assume that every person you meet, you will see again in the future. If you miss a person's name when you are introduced, force yourself to politely ask again. It shows that you are interested. Then say the person's name at least five times to yourself. Continually use his or her name when speaking to the person. This will reinforce your memory. Remember, people's names are the labels given to them by their mothers and fathers. Names are important, and when you open a conversation by using a person's name, that person gains a great deal of respect for you.

When you remember a person's name, it starts off the next conversation you have with that person on a more meaningful level. Did you ever get into bed on a cold night and the sheets were freezing? You had to lie there for some time in the cold until your body warmed up the sheets, right? Forgetting a person's name makes you go through that warming-up period. Be a warm, cozy bed sheet for people by remembering their names and a few simple facts about them.

3. Get enthused about other people's claims to fame. Something that N. Thusiastic knows, which I.M. Dull does not know, is the secret of getting enthused about people's accomplishments by their standards, not ours. A conversation overheard in a university lunchroom demonstrates this point. The dialogue was between a professor and Jeffrey, a student who apparently was not in this particular professor's class.

> *Jeffrey:* "I received my grades today, and I got a D in my Elements of Geography class."
> *Dr. Livingood:* "I'm sorry to hear that news."
> *Jeffrey:* "Why? I thought I was going to fail, which would have meant that I could not graduate in June. All I needed was the D to receive my university degree."

Dr. Livingood made the error of judging the student's accomplishment by a professor's standards. Perhaps the professor was an A student throughout his schooling. Or perhaps he judged the student's accomplishment by more universal standards, where a C is the average grade. Either way, the professor missed the opportunity to be a stimulant. He forgot to consider the grade from Jeffrey's point of view. Thus, he failed to recognize Jeffrey's great accomplishment: he will be a university graduate.

4. Make it a point to help every person you meet to feel important and significant. People have no greater need than the need to "count." Apathy, low morale, stagnation, loneliness, and even suicide are symptoms of people who are basically saying, "I don't count. The world doesn't need me. It doesn't even matter whether or not I wake up tomorrow morning." Every person you see walking down the street, every person you meet at a social gathering, every person you work with has in common the need to count. Enthusiastically count them in.

One of our close friends, Dr. Richard Cahn, knows as much about improving employee morale in an organization as perhaps anyone in the world. Dick, as of this writing, is superintendent of one of the larger school systems in the eastern United States. Dick was elected to his position during a time when the schools were facing several major problems, especially in areas of poor employee morale, excessive professional burnout, and seemingly irreversible financial problems. Very few people would even want that challenge. However, Dick loves a challenge and is one of the most naturally enthusiastic people you could meet. He met the challenge squarely and in only one year—that's right, one year—turned the school district into a place where teachers wanted to be, where students took pride in being, and where new ideas flowed like the winds of Wyoming. It was the first time that the teachers' contract was signed before the beginning of the school year (incidentally, it was a three-year contract!).

How did Dick achieve these Herculean accomplishments? Dick, in a humble tone, would tell you, "Working with people is the easiest task in the world if you just remember what makes people tick. People need to count, to feel a part of the organization, and to see that they make a difference. When I'm with a person, that individual is the only important person in the world and I have nothing else on my mind. Nothing else matters at that moment."

Employing enthusiasm and encouragement in his organization, Dick bubbles as he shares his beliefs about people in general. The master builder of morale reflects, "It has been my observation that most people are more fulfilled by performing well rather than by performing poorly, by contributing rather than by being uncooperative, and by feeling recognized rather than by feeling insignificant. People can find this fulfillment when an encouraging atmosphere exists. When we enthusiastically look for the best in people, we more often than not get their best. The indisputable principle of encouragement is, 'What you see is what you get.'"

When you get enthused about people, you turn them on and you reap the rewards of seeing their fires for life lit again. Be a stimulant by: (1) getting enthused about other people's lives, (2) seeing what's right with people, (3) remembering every person's name and a few facts about the person, (4) recognizing every person's claims to fame, and finally (5) helping every single person to feel significant and to have the "I count" feeling.

After putting on your positive, enthusiastic spectacles and getting enthused about yourself and other people, develop your self-image even further by getting enthused about life today and learning to appreciate the beauty that surrounds you.

Get Enthused About Life!

Celebrate today! We are now living in the greatest time ever. People perched on the porch of pessimism selectively perceive only the negative. They suffer from perceptual myopia, a disease character-ized by the symptoms of negativism and blame. They miss all of the great news dancing in front of their eyes. They miss the fact that probably 5.5 billion out of the 6 billion people in the world would trade places with them in a moment's notice. What's worse, they miss making the best of their lives and being who they are. Put on your enthusiastic glasses and get high not only on yourself and other people, but on life itself.

Instead of life as we know it today, would you rather be fighting dinosaurs? Would you prefer coping with freezing weather by rub-bing two sticks together just to get a fleeting spark. If you would prefer getting warm that way, we have great news—you still have that option! Instead of the conveniences of life today, would you prefer having an outhouse for your bathroom? Would you rather use a scrub board to clean your clothing?

Would you rather have the mobility we enjoy today or be restricted to a turtle as the only form of transportation? Again, you still have most of these options available to you. However, although modern conveniences may not be the answer to everything, they certainly make life more comfortable and allow you more time for your loved ones, religion, business, and/or leisure.

People who glorify the past are selective in their visions. They choose the positive elements from their imaginary ideal but ignore most of the dismal aspects about the past. So, enthusiastically click your feet together and rejoice about the beauty of life by seeing what's right instead of what's wrong with the present. You are living in the greatest time ever and things are going to get even better. Because of enthusiasts, we are only a few years away from a pill that will enable you to eat anything you want without gaining a single pound. We are a short time away from a nasal spray that will enhance your memory. Because of optimists, we are only a brief period of time away from taking partial control of some forms of destructive thundershowers and hurricanes. We are only a little calendar distance from the time when the average human being will live to be 100. And soon we will even have control over most forms of tooth decay.

Remember, not one of these breakthroughs came from the mind of a pessimist. Rejoice about the beauty of living in today's world and shout about the even greater beauty of living in tomorrow's world. Enthusiasm is the only way to go to achieve success. Reach Success City by developing your positive self-image fueled by enthusiasm.

A Lifetime Of Success Is Yours With Creativity And Enthusiasm

Success is the product of the creation of new ideas combined with the enthusiasm it takes to make these ideas happen. You can achieve any goal and succeed at anything you do just by continuously reminding yourself to see things in refreshing ways and to become enthusiastic about life, other people, and, mainly, yourself.

Don't just saunter through life. Step through your day with a brisk pace. Own your life. Make things happen. When you get high on life, you can change the world. Imagine what could be accomplished in just one day of your life with the powers of your enthusiasm.

> In one day, you could have breakfast in New York City, lunch in Vancouver, British Columbia, and settle down for a roast pig dinner in Honolulu.

> In one day, you could travel one-seventh of the way to the moon. But if you don't have a full two weeks to spend traveling to and from the moon, just wait. In the oncoming years, it will take even less of your valuable "alive" time.

In one day, you could produce the beginnings of a new life.

In one day, you could put a smile on hundreds of faces.

In one day, Mother Theresa, the Nobel Peace Prize winner, feeds tens of thousands of children in India.

In one day, in fact in only seven seconds, the pit crew at an Indianapolis 500 race can change all of the tires on a car.

Ignite your enthusiasm—the power system to success. Think of the possibilities you have in just one day when you are enthusiastic. What could you possibly do with your unlimited talents, unlimited assets, unlimited creative ideas, unlimited enthusiasm in only one day? Well, brace yourself; not only do you have one of these days available to you, you probably have 30,000 or more of these days available in your lifetime.

Application Of Enthusiasm Skills

1. Enthusiasm is not something a person is born with. Enthusiasm is a characteristic available to anyone. How do you become enthusiastic? Simple. **Become enthusiastic!**

2. You can develop your positive self-image by developing your enthusiasm for yourself, other people, and life. By developing this enthusiasm, you become more positive toward life, and as a result, you become more popular and a more rewarding person to be near.

3. Get high on other people. Be easy to be with and give people that "around the fireplace," relaxed feeling.

4. See what's right with yourself. Do an asset analysis of yourself every day.

5. As we look at the history of humankind, it was always the enthusiastic, hopeful people who made the difference. Make the positive difference wherever you go and spread the contagion of enthusiasm.

References

Ellis, Albert and Robert Harper. *A New Guide to Rational Living*. North Hollywood, CA: Wilshire Books, 1975.

Zastrow, Charles. *Talk to Yourself*. Englewood Cliffs, NJ: Prentice Hall, 1978.

9 Focusing On Assets, Strengths & Resources

Relationships that are negative and fault-finding discourage and reduce an individual's energy as well as the desire to cooperate. In contrast, focusing on assets, strengths, and resources encourages and energizes.

Murray is a manager who has a natural bent for focusing on the positive. He's never seen a liability or deficit that couldn't be turned into a possibility.

Betty, from the secretarial pool, is working with him this week. She has been with a number of critical managers and is overly cautious. She is now making a number of typing errors as well as misfiling. Murray notices her outstanding method of working with people on the telephone. That's what he discusses with her at the end of the day. She feels recognized and appreciated. The next day, feeling less stress, she reduces her mistakes.

At home, Murray's wife is always complaining about Sue, 17, and Henry, 16. Murray, instead, focuses on Sue's responsibility and Henry's willingness to help. Murray's style of relationship accentuates the positive, and people love to work with him.

Encouragement provides alternative ways of looking at and understanding oneself. Discouragement is primarily the result of having a constricted perspective on life. The encourager works to expand the narrow vision of the person in order to develop a greater range and variety of responses to the challenges of living. Always begin by identifying a person's assets. When an individual is not functioning, most often we tend to be focused on identifying weaknesses, limitations, and what's wrong. The mistaken assumption is that we help people by pointing out their weaknesses.

If you have been in a relationship that focused on pointing out the weaknesses and mistakes of the other person, you know this becomes competitive and painful. You cannot improve a relationship or change a person's behavior through fault-finding and attacking. While the intention may be to improve the other person, the end result is that the other person becomes resistant, discouraged, and uncooperative.

Identifying assets is similar to rooting for the home team. Even though, in the past, the New York Mets, the San Diego Padres, and the Sacramento Kings have shown far more weaknesses than strengths, a loyal fan finds certain strengths—reasons to continue to root for the team.

How proficient are you at identifying your own assets? What do you like about yourself? What do you feel are your strengths, or the things you do well? Are you an asset-finder in contrast to a fault-finder? Are you able to find assets in your relationships? Can you go beyond the way a person seems to be and instead look for the hidden treasure, the person's strengths. Strengths may not appear on the surface because the person is afraid to show them.

Turning Liabilities Into Assets

The encourager is a person with a natural bent, an interest, and excitement in finding ways to turn a liability into an asset. In professional basketball, a high percentage of players are anywhere from 6'4" to 7'6" in height. However, other players are relatively short. Two of these shorter players are Mugsy Bogues and Spud Webb. They have managed to take their liability, the lack of height, and turn it into an asset. They are actually very difficult to guard because of their lack of height. They appear to go under and around the taller players.

Look at some of the liabilities you see in people around you. A shy person or a perfectionist could take that liability and turn it into an asset. For example, the perfectionist could shift his or her focus and could be perfectly imperfect, making mistakes without any fear of criticism. The courage to be imperfect means you make mistakes because you are human. It's not a liability or limitation; it's just a reality and can be accepted.

Each of us has goals, certain things we want to accomplish and move toward. Goals may be social, personal, or professional. Identify how your assets can be used more effectively in helping you achieve your goals.

Discovering The Hidden Resources

You need to become increasingly aware of how you can get in touch with resources that are just under the surface of your list of talents. These resources tend to not come out because you work in places where you feel safe and secure, and you don't necessarily stretch to reach them.

An essential encouragement skill is being able to spotlight and magnify an individual's strengths, assets, and resources. We all know people who are "nit-pickers" or "flaw-finders." They can always spot a mistake, a weakness, or something which isn't as it should be. They are often quick to offer their criticism. We suggest the opposite side of this polarity—becoming an individual who is find-tuned to hearing and seeing resources. As you train yourself to see the inherent potential and good in a person, you are stimulating the ability to encourage.

In the following exercises, you will have an opportunity to assess your ability to focus on strengths, assets, and resources.

Situation 1.   Sam is quiet, reserved, shy, and often late in meeting his commitments. The people he knows have come to believe he won't contribute much, but he *will* contribute. What do his resources seem to be?

Situation 2.   Mrs. Jackson is an attractive woman with a violent temper and a tendency to overreact to anything that doesn't go smoothly. She becomes upset so quickly, regularly, and vigorously that her husband and children always approach her very cautiously. What might her resources be?

Situation 3.   Jack has been referred to the counselor because he is uninvolved in his classes and lacks interest in his grades in high school. Jack has average ability, is easy going and cooperative with his parents, and presents few other problems.

The youngest of three children, Jack is 16. His sister is 29 and his brother is 35. Because he is so much younger than his siblings, Jack has been raised as an only child and is accustomed to getting his way.

Jack is socially cooperative and interested in athletics, and he has a group of close friends. His parents are distressed about his lack of involvement in school work. What are Jack's strengths and resources for meeting his academic challenges?

Our world provides us with a great variety of stimuli which come to us through a range of sensory modalities. This necessitates learning to focus on certain stimuli while ignoring others. Discouraged people have learned to focus on what they find to be deficient, defective, and a liability. In their own behavior they are most in touch with their own weaknesses and liabilities. When they are in contact with other people, they maintain their discouraged outlook and quickly spot deficiencies.

Situation 4.   Fred is a contractor. He is the middle child of three and feels he has not done as well as his older brother, a lawyer, or his younger brother, a physician. In his view, "the world is unfair" and he hasn't received the recognition and rewards he should. This influences him to choose a pessimistic view of life.

This view is reflected in his family life. He regularly corrects his wife about her cooking and social relationships, and his children are subjected to his demands to excel.

The tradespeople and salesmen who work with Fred have little respect for him and try to avoid anything but casual contact. Fred is always quick to point out defects in their workmanship or the products they sell.

What is Fred's focus? What does he get for it?

Situation 5.   Lucy is the supervisor on a production line in a small plant. She originally took the job to supplement her family's income but has stayed on because she likes being in control. While management thinks highly of Lucy, her fellow workers find her surly, demanding, and fault-finding. They feel oppressed by her superior attitude and her condescending manner and have negative feelings about her.

Lucy brings this attitude home with her. She lets her husband know she is a supporter of the family, and in many ways he feels "supervised." The children see their mother as someone who is nagging, fault-finding, and overly demanding.

What is Lucy's focus? What does she get for it?

Situation 6.   Ralph sells medical supplies. He has a large territory and many contacts. He has a positive outlook and communicates his faith in and respect for others. Because he thinks in a positive vein, he is usually looking for the strengths, assets, and resources that exist in others. He can quickly identify the reliability of the newspaper carrier, the helpfulness of his children, the courtesy of a neighbor, the enthusiasm of a competitor, the agility of his tennis opponent, and the caring of his wife. When you are with Ralph, you always know where you stand. He communicates positively how he experiences you. You also usually feel uplifted because Ralph tends to raise your spirits.

What is Ralph's focus? What does he get for it?

Situation 7.   Wayne is a pastor who relates well with people. He is genuinely interested in their welfare, and it shows. When he greets people as they come to church, he makes eye contact and looks for their good points. Among the membership, he is able to perceive how individuals can take a liability and turn it into an asset. He even plays games in which members consider traits that could be turned from liabilities into resources; for example, stubbornness could be determination or commitment.

His sermons frequently focus on how members can be aware of their assets and how they can start to look for resources in others.

What is Wayne's focus? What does he give to others through his focus?

As we follow the stories of people who are encouraged, you begin to see how they differ from people who are discouraged. Their perception of life is more positive; they are a greater joy to be around, and they uplift you by their presence. Your burdens feel lighter and you move with more hope because they increase your courage.

The traditional focus of psychology was to diagnose by assessing liabilities and determining what was wrong with the client. The model followed the medical model and sought to understand pathology and weakness.

However, if you are trying to relate more effectively to your spouse, child, friend, colleague, or acquaintance, will you relate more effectively by identifying and focusing on what is wrong or what is right? The classic mother-in-law joke portrays a fault-finding relationship, although this may be a difficult situation. However, how many of our relationships tend to be negative, fault-finding, destructive, or perhaps neutral, lacking the positive affirmation we have been discussing?

In the medical model of understanding patients, doctors are

usually better trained to deal with sickness than to help you become healthy. Health is more than freedom from disease. The holistic doctor sees health as a positive attribute. This doctor is able to help you expand your world, for as you become well, you are not only free of illness but can live more vibrantly.

We are encouraging you to become a more encouraging person not only for what it will do for others, but for what it will do for you. As you begin to look for resources, focus on the positive, and affirm others, you will have a phenomenal experience. You will have joined the encouragers and resigned from the discouragers!

In your next contacts with people, think of them as truly precious gifts placed in your presence for affirmation. Then, since your task is to affirm, begin to consider a potential area in which you might affirm: ideas, attitudes, feelings, physical attributes, or talents. Now that you have reoriented your thinking from that of a fault-finder or a neutral observer, you will be surprised at how much there is to affirm. As you affirm, you will be pleased to observe the other person's inner glow, which makes it possible to identify even more things to affirm.

For the moment, identify someone you know reasonably well. Decide you want to improve your relationship and want to find ways to encourage that person. How will you begin? If you are thinking positively, you will have established some traits you can readily observe and affirm.

When you have difficulty identifying a positive trait or resource, identify the source of your difficulty. Often, you will find you are discouraged about the task of diagnosing strengths and resources. Your own high standards may influence you to look for especially outstanding traits. Your over-ambition also influences you to look for the outstanding, the excellent, and to overlook resources that are apparent once you refocus. High standards not only block relationships and communication, but they actually color our perception so that we miss the beautiful but often less obvious in our world.

Have you ever walked or bicycled on the same path a number of times and then one day been impressed by the shape of a tree or the colors in nature? They were there all the time, but your preoccupation kept you from opening your perceptions.

Think of someone close to you—a spouse, a child, a friend. You know their obvious assets and talents. List them here.

Now go on a treasure hunt. Discover the buried gold. Find a trait the person close to you has that you have not considered but which is undoubtedly a hidden treasure or resource. It may be something you were not aware of before or something that was always there but unrecognized. What have you discovered?

If you had difficulty discovering traits that are assets and potential resources, do you recognize how much of that difficulty may be due to the limitations you place on your talent search because you have trained yourself to see the negative and to be fault-finding?

You can become a great help and a gift to others as you improve your vision. It is like going to the eye doctor to get your first pair of glasses or have your prescription changed. You now have a much sharper perspective of your world. You, too, can change your view of the world as you decide to look for resources and be less concerned with deficits.

Review the following list of traits which many might consider undesirable or to be avoided. See whether you can determine how each trait can be an asset.

Trait	Turned Into Asset
Stubborn	
Talkative	
Bossy	
Nosy	
Socially aggressive	

Here are some ways to turn these traits into assets:

Stubborn	Persistent, determined
Talkative	Informative, friendly
Bossy	Taking charge, in control
Nosy	Inquisitive, concerned
Socially aggressive	Fun to be with

Now list some questionable traits of people you are familiar with and identify ways to turn these traits into assets.

Trait   *Turned Into Asset*

What we are suggesting is that you train yourself to become a talent scout. The professional talent scout must be able to envision the potential of a person with additional training and maturity. The talent scout searches for talent in the raw or diamonds in the rough. Companies that drill for natural resources must be able to judge from the surface and from samples whether a site has the potential to be productive.

Each of us has the innate potential to become all we are intended to become. However, we need to be nourished. Too often, we consider nourishment to be primarily physical. The human being needs the psychological nourishment which comes from support, acceptance, and encouragement.

As you train yourself to find neglected resources and traits that need to be released, *you* become a valued resource to another person. Your ability to find previously overlooked traits helps that person to feel newly valued.

To do this well, you have to feel good about yourself. What you are able to do for others—accept, value, enhance, and affirm—you must also do for yourself.

As part of your personal talent and resource survey, identify your strengths and assets (minimum of five):

Now identify some or your resources and assets that are not generally known. These are the traits you keep under cover. You seldom use or reveal them, but they have great potential for enhancing your life or the lives of others. List these resources:

Perhaps you, like most people, have forgotten how many assets and positive points you have. Your constricted viewpoint of yourself has often discouraged you, but by recognizing your strengths you can again realize your positive complexity.

Application Of Focusing On Strengths, Assets, And Resources

Situation 1.   Timmy, age 14, says, "I lost in the bowling finals. I could have been the best in my school but in the last game I messed up. Boy, am I bad under pressure!"

Your response:

Situation 2.   You are a school counselor. A teenager named Mark has just been referred to you. Mark turned himself in to the principal for using different techniques to steal exams from teachers and selling them to his classmates. He has just received sermons from the principal, two of his teachers, his parents, and his minister. How will you deal with Mark, keeping in mind the skill of focusing on resources?

Your response:

Situation 3.   Your seven-year-old son started a fight with two ten-year-olds in the neighborhood because he said they called you a bad name. How would you approach your son?
Your response:

10 Perceptual Alternative Skills

F red is fired from a job where he had worked his way up to a top line supervisor. The firing was not anticipated. People at work are very sympathetic. They explain to him how unfair they think this it and they know how bad he must be feeling. His wife is concerned about the impact this will have on him.

Fred is someone who regularly uses perceptual alternatives. He gives his own unique meaning to any specific event. Although the firing may be seen as a rejection, a downer, a disaster, he decides to see it differently. He views it as an opportunity. He can take his supervisory skills and use them in some other endeavor. However, before he does that, he will give serious consideration to doing something he has always hoped he could do.

He has always had an interest in golf. He has learned that the supervising manager at the local golf course is retiring. Fred has played a lot, knows the people at the course, and feels he could do a good job. He turns what could be a negative into a positive. He views the possibilities in a situation and moves toward them. It's not that he ignores the down side, but he doesn't become discouraged about losing his job. He quickly shifts to an encouraging perceptual alternative.

In this chapter, you will learn a number of ways to switch from discouraging to encouraging perceptual alternatives.

Often when you hear people complaining, it sounds as if they are the victim of circumstances beyond their control. Consider what part people play in how things go for them. For example, a person may talk about how difficult things are at home with an adolescent who is rebellious, a young child who has difficulties in school, and a wife who is uncooperative. This person seems to be experiencing disrespect and a total lack of cooperation in every area of his or her family life. When you listen, you need to identify the part the person plays in the problem. How is she or he creating ineffective relationships? Why are people no longer cooperating with him or her? What could he or she do to improve relationships with friends and family and at work? A person doesn't merely behave, but feels, thinks, and decides and has goals and values. To really understand each other, we need to have insight into these qualities, because they influence our choice of alternatives.

Perceptual alternatives are different ways of viewing and giving meaning to the same situation (Losoncy, 1977). When we become aware of perceptual alternatives, we are more in control of our options. We are able to choose how to interpret an event and how to behave. To heighten your awareness, consider the variety of ways of viewing and interpreting the following events.

Fred, age seven, receives a low grade on his arithmetic paper. Many of us would say he will feel discouraged, disappointed, or angry. If he's not overly concerned with grades, he may not be upset. His goal may be to show his teacher or his parents that they cannot do anything to make him work. The teachers, the parents, and the child each have a different way of viewing the low grade in arithmetic. The differences are based on the creative capacity of each person to give their own meaning to any event (i.e., a perceptual alternative).

Mary has been counting on going to dinner and a show on Friday night. Ron, her boyfriend, calls and says that something has come up and he can't make it. He apologizes and says he'll call her back when he can find another time to get together. Mary could feel disappointed, rejected, frustrated, and angry. However, if she sees Ron's change of plans as unfortunate instead of a catastrophe, she can start to plan how she will spend the evening and find something enjoyable to do. You choose how you respond to and interpret any given event. The more perceptual alternatives you develop, the more capable you are of dealing with the stresses of life.

In other words, "If life gives you lemons, make lemonade." Let's see how you can have a positive attitude in some different situations. How might the following events be interpreted in a discouraging way or, by contrast, in an encouraging way?

Bill loses in the third set of a tennis match in which he was playing one of the best players in the area.
Discouraging perceptual alternative:

Encouraging perceptual alternative:

Your son calls to indicate he won't be home from college for the holidays because he has too many incompletes and has to stay to make them up.
Discouraging perceptual alternative:

Encouraging perceptual alternative:

Your husband has been building up his law practice and now has a very heavy load of clients. He calls and says that he has lost one of his most lucrative clients.
Discouraging perceptual alternative:

Encouraging perceptual alternative:

Your wife has been very active in many organizations and has anticipated being selected to join a certain club. She tells you she was passed over for a younger woman.

Discouraging perceptual alternative:

Encouraging perceptual alternative:

Clearly, you have options about what you choose to see. You actually produce your experiences. Although there are numerous ways of interpreting any given situation, it is the meaning you give to a situation that determines its effect upon you.

In general, a situation does not directly cause a feeling. How you interpret the meaning of a situation influences the development of a feeling. Even in a situation as serious as death, a person with hope can find reason to rejoice. The tinge of sadness some parents experience as a child begins school or leaves home for college can be balanced by the joy of recognizing that the child is maturing or the parents anticipating that they will have more time to themselves.

The encouraging person has the ability to view the same situation in several ways. The more ways of viewing the world you possess, the greater your capacities for adjusting to life. Your ability to develop perceptual alternatives is closely linked to your willingness to take risks and grow. A courageous lifestyle, which is an essential element of being encouraging, stimulates the individual to see risk taking as a rewarding way of life.

It is important to deal with life's challenges as if there is a solution. Once you are solution-oriented, you are in a position to see a variety of possibilities. However, if you are only problem-focused, you may quickly become discouraged.

Increasing Your Perceptual Alternatives

The discouraged person thinks, "This is the way things are and I can't do anything about it." Whether the situation is physical, social, or intellectual, the discouraged person approaches it fatalistically and pessimistically. The encouraging person, on the other hand, is one who sees the rainbow that follows the storm and finds something potentially good in even the worst situation.

Consider the following ways to develop perceptual alternatives:

1. Think of the last time you felt you were being treated unfairly by a relative, friend, salesperson, or stranger. Recall why you felt you were treated unfairly.

   Consider why the other person behaved that way. Be empathic. See things from his or her perspective.

   There are many viewpoints on an issue, in some cases as many as there are people. A position is seldom entirely right or entirely wrong. There are usually more grays than whites or blacks when we look at opinions on an issue.

2. You finally extend yourself to somebody you have been wanting to become acquainted with and are snubbed. You feel humiliated. You can view this experience in a number of ways, including:

   "I knew it would never work."

   "They think they are too good for me."

   "Getting around and socializing isn't for me; I'm better off sticking with people I know."

   "I probably misunderstood this person and expected too much. I'll be more patient the next time I approach a new person."

   "Maybe the person has a fear of getting close."

   Which of these answers most likely fits your way of responding?

   In any response, remember that you have more alternatives than your first, instantaneous response. As you pause, you permit the perceptual alternatives to emerge. This gives you more ways to respond.

Developing the ability to expand your perceptual alternatives is very important in increasing your ability to encourage. Insofar as you are able to perceive a variety of ways of looking at a situation, you become more likely to see the encouraging side of any situation. Perceptual alternatives enable you to be aware of the feelings, purpose, and potential that lie just beneath the surface of an individual. By utilizing your perceptual alternatives, you can see beauty in what appears to be the ordinary. You can hear the positive feelings and caring behind the angry shout, and you can touch the softness that may be masked by the cold, sullen stare.

Your senses are another door to developing perceptual alternatives. For example, Jenny says, "I don't care. Do whatever you want to." She sounds angry but you can also hear her disappointment, frustration, and rejection. You could respond angrily, but you decide to respond to what you hear by saying, "You don't think I care about you." This response can open up a totally different conversation.

When you increase your capacity to develop perceptual alternatives, you are more capable of encouraging.

Your daughter gets average grades in school and provides little opportunity for you to be encouraging in that area. You have been inclined to focus on weaknesses and mistakes but decide to look at the positive side of her behavior (Dinkmeyer and McKay, 1976). This brings your attention to the child's outgoing, helpful nature and the easygoing way she carries on relationships with siblings, parents, and friends. Without developing an alternative way of perceiving your child, you have been caught in your limited view of believing she is not adequate academically.

We may have preconceived ideas about people. What perceptions and meanings come to mind when you hear the following words:

Teacher   Dentist   Lawyer   Accountant   Policeman

Jew   Catholic   Wasp   Baptist

Have you ever met anyone who is the exact opposite of your stereotype? For each word above, think of some traits that are more positive.

The goal of an encouraging person is to be open, to see more perceptions and alternatives, and to see something positive in anything.

Your ability to encourage is enhanced through the expansion of **social interest**. As Adler (1939) explained, social interest is the capacity to participate in the give and take of life, to be more interested in others than in self, and to be identified with humankind in contrast to feeling as if one is working against people. Social interest is a criterion for healthy psychological development. Those who lack social interest tend to be self-centered, uncooperative, and delinquent.

You are more likely to encourage when you have high self-esteem and feel good about yourself. When you have self-esteem, there is less need to focus on your faults and be overly concerned about mistakes. The encouraging person most likely will interpret mistakes as merely guidelines to improve performance. Self-esteem enables the encouraging person to feel more confident about self and hence more free to respond positively.

What are some indications of your social interest? What would you do to expand your social interest?

What are some indications of your self-esteem? What do you do regularly to expand another's feelings of self-worth?

What are some ways you use your perceptual alternatives?

Think about three people you know. Take some time to consider the traits you feel they have and write them down.

Person A:

Person B:

Person C:

Do you usually look for and identify the positive or negative aspects of a situation? Are you more aware of the positive or negative traits in a person? What habits prevent your ability to encourage?

When you primarily identify negative characteristics in others, it doesn't mean they are inept or ineffective. It may mean your focus is negative. If you train yourself primarily to identify negative traits, you will find it nearly impossible to encourage. The encouraging person has developed the ability to identify and focus on positive qualities and to express those positive observations to another.

Think about a person you have difficulty getting along with. Some of the clash is due to traits you find offensive. Mentally, move those traits into the background; now focus on identifying the person's positive qualities. Through this exercise, you convince yourself that by perceiving alternatives you can change perceptions. You now have a key to becoming a more encouraging person.

Suppose you have difficulty getting along with the following people. Move the negative traits to the background and focus only on the person's positive qualities.

1. The nagging neighbor

2. The noisy children in your neighborhood

3. Your demanding boss

4. Your constantly complaining spouse

5. Someone who is difficult to get along with

Once you are able to identify positive traits, the next step is to express your positive observations. You have undoubtedly had practice expressing your negative evaluations and feelings to others. Experience in complaining and fault-finding is not uncommon: "You're late again." "Will you ever grow up?" "This report is inadequate." "If you'd only practice more, your Spanish would improve." This type of conversation seldom, if ever, improves a relationship. Instead, it tends to damage a relationship and you find yourself ignored.

You might find that expressing positive feelings brings rewarding results. Comments such as "I like..." or "You're doing much better at..." or "You seem to be enjoying..." will undoubtedly be well received.

It is up to you to find meaning in life. This meaning can be encouraging, uplifting, and stimulating, or it can be discouraging, devaluing, and devastating. The choice is yours. You will see for yourself the rewards and positive feelings that come from being encouraging. It's all in how you decide to see it. What personal power!

Application Of Using Perceptual Alternatives

Situation 1. Choose a historical figure, movie star, sports figure, or anyone about whom you know a lot.

A. Write a few sentences describing the negative traits and characteristics of this person.

B. Write a few sentences describing the positive traits and characteristics of this person.

Situation 2.   Think about yourself.

A. Write a few sentences describing your positive traits and characteristics.

B. Write a few sentences describing your negative traits and characteristics.

Situation 3.   The following circumstance might at first be viewed negatively. Through the use of perceptual alternatives, can you find some positive ways of viewing this event?

Ted and Sally decide to break off their three-year engagement. It is painful for both of them. What are some perceptual alternatives? How might this be helpful to both of them?

My Plan For Becoming More Encouraging

My assets as an encourager:

Things that restrict me from being more encouraging:

Responses that interfere with my being encouraging:

I am becoming less:

Demanding	Threatening
Correcting	Punishing
Lecturing	Other

My progress this week:	More	Less	Changed

Listening to feelings

Responding congruently

Showing genuine enthusiasm

Focusing on resources

Helping others see alternatives

Seeing the humor in a situation

Focusing on efforts

Combating discouraging beliefs

Encouraging commitment

Encouraging mutual feedback

Being respectful

What I learned about myself:

References

Adler, Alfred. *Social Interest.* New York: Greenberg Press, 1939.

Dinkmeyer, Don and Gary McKay. *Systematic Training for Effective Parenting.* Circle Pines, MN: American Guidance Service, 1976.

Losoncy, Lewis. *Turning People On.* New York: Simon & Schuster, 1977.

11   Humor Skills To Lighten Things Up

We are all acquainted with the topic of humor. Usually we think of comedians as creating humor. The humor skills we are talking about in this chapter are different. These humor skills suggest that you see humor in your mistakes, your erroneous beliefs, and your habits which may constrict you from getting the most out of your life.

A sense of humor helps people see what is funny in a situation. Sometimes when bad things happen to good people, we have a hard time seeing anything funny. However, we can begin to see some alternatives that are possible in a situation.

Larry is presenting a lecture on "The Courage to Be Imperfect." He wants to do a good job because he thinks the topic has great significance for his audience. As he begins the lecture, he says he will be talking about "The Courage to Be Perfect." He catches his mistake and corrects himself. He then illustrates the basic concepts of humor. As he talks, he presents a story intended to be humorous, but it is not perceived that way by the audience. He finds humor in his inability to make his point.

We all have different views of what is humorous. Many of us find it easy to laugh at jokes, sitcoms, comedians, and mistakes that others make, but fail to see any humor in ourselves or any mistake we make. Instead, if we make a mistake, we tend to feel embarrassed and humiliated and certainly are not able to laugh at ourselves. This defensiveness tends to lead to being uptight and tense, which leads to other mistakes. Humor, however, enables people to see their humanness and to accept themselves as imperfect.

Mature people not only see humor in the events around them but, even more important, are able to laugh at themselves. A sense of humor can actually change your perspective and your frame of mind, so that when someone makes a mistake, although you may be disappointed or concerned, you can also realize that it is not a disaster.

Everything has meaning insofar as we give it meaning. Humor is a sense of perspective which helps us recognize that almost everything can be seen and understood differently. Humor is the ability to develop perceptual alternatives—to shift one's perspective from pain to pleasure, from total anger to feeling upset. In other words, you modify your perceptual and emotional response. When you have this humorous attitude, you are capable of creating unique, joyful experiences. Humor becomes a state of mind that frees you from discouragement, depression, loneliness, rejection, and all the other negative emotions that accompany a discouraged outlook on life.

Your sense of humor enables you to see what is funny in a situation. You also recognize your weaknesses and imperfections without being overwhelmed by them. The ability to accept your imperfections and your mistakes helps you live with less tension and with greater freedom and self-acceptance.

If you are discouraged, you may look at problems in such a way that you become mired in them. Mentally you might say that you are on a "humor-free" diet. You view everything you see seriously. This blocks you from seeing the alternatives, especially the humorous ones.

With a sense of humor, you are able to see the alternatives that are possible in a situation. You are able to release some of the burden of the negatives as you recognize other possible ways to respond.

Humor gives you the ability to switch your frame of reference. You become able to find other ways to view the same situation. You don't just see the "down" side, you see the potential "up" side. You don't only see the sadness, you see hope. You have a picture that is much more vivid with a greater number of alternatives. Once you let go of your faulty beliefs, mistaken ideas, and your own ego, which constricts you, you are free to see the alternatives. Humor opens up your thought processes and encourages your creativity.

Humor is a powerful agent for change. It actually refocuses your attention away from the upsetting nature of a particular situation and helps you see other ways to interpret the situation. Humor is also effective with very strong emotions, such as fear and rage. You cannot focus on incompatible feelings at the same time. When humor prevails, fear and rage cannot co-exist.

A sense of humor is natural in some people and needs to be cultivated in others. For those who want to improve their sense of humor, the following might be effective:

1. Adopt a more playful, carefree attitude, which permits you to be silly, humorous, and relaxed.

2. Appreciate the paradoxes in your life, the ways in which you present a front to protect your real self from being seen.

3. Laugh at yourself and see yourself in perspective. Accept your own imperfections and mistakes.

Do you often find yourself in situations in which you have very rigid and restricted perceptions of yourself, others, and life? This is because your self-constrictive approach produces this limited point of view.

The humorist, a person who sees things in perspective, raises some of the following paradoxes (O'Connell, 1995):

1. Demonstrate to me logically how stupid you are.

2. Show how you are a victim of your past moments and that your present moments don't count if your present moments will someday become your past.

3. Demonstrate to me perfectly how imperfect you are.

4. Create further proof that you can't create.

The Worst Of The Most Horrible Things That Could Happen

Discouraged people think in terms of superlatives such as "I am the worst" or "The most horrible thing that could ever happen is..." However, they seldom confront or recognize the worst. Discouraged people remain foggy about what could happen. As long as they are confused, they have an ideal excuse for remaining immobilized and not taking action.

The humorist helps people explore and confront "the worst." In this process, people begin to realize that "the worst" is unlikely to occur to that degree, and if it does, it will be possible to adjust and act accordingly. In their humorous book *How to Make Yourself Miserable*, Dan Greenberg and Marcia Jacobs (1966) suggest that most worriers are amateurs at finding ways to help people become more creative worriers. For example, a common worry is anxiety about one's health. Even if you have had a medical exam in the last three months, can you be free of worry? Consider some of the possibilities.

First of all, how can you be sure some serious condition hasn't cropped up since your examination? Second, how can you be sure there wasn't some fact you neglected to tell the doctor, something you didn't think was important enough to mention at the time, but which any doctor would instantly recognize as the tip-off to a problem?

Assuming there wasn't a single relevant fact you failed to tell the doctor, how can you be absolutely certain the doctor was competent enough to interpret the information correctly? How can you be sure the doctor gave you a complete physical examination? How complete is a complete physical examination? Couldn't there have been a test—perhaps the very one which would have revealed your illness—that the doctor didn't consider worth giving you because the illness was too rare and the test too cumbersome?

Did the doctor, for example, give you a complete set of x-rays, including a G.I. series? If not, that's probably the only thing that could have saved you.

Let's even say that you're positive you didn't move while the plate was being exposed. How can you be sure that your x-rays weren't accidentally switched with those of a healthy person by some young intern in the darkroom who was simultaneously developing stag films?

In short, there is no situation that cannot be turned into a true worry with the application of a little creative negative thinking.

Sue wanted to dance. At the same time, she was afraid to ask Bill whether he would dance with her because believed he would turn her down. She went for a long time without realizing that fear kept her from living her life more fully. The encourager asks Sue to write down the chain of events that could occur if the worst thing did happen.

> "I would ask him and he would turn me down."

> "He would tell everyone he knows that he rejected me. This would include advertising in all the major newspapers, TV programs, and radio stations throughout the country."

> "Wherever I would go, people would know me as the terrible person who was rejected by Bill."

> "No one would ever again dance with me since they wouldn't want to be seen with anyone so horrible."

> "I would have to live out my life by myself, with no friends and in total worthlessness from this one rejection."

The encourager continues, "As a worthless, no-good person with no friends, banished to your house forever, what are some things you still could do?"

> *Sue:* "Well, I enjoy reading and TV. Maybe I could do a little writing. Maybe I could write about a life of being worthless and make money on it—since I would be so famous. I can see it now, 'I Was The World's Most Rejected Person.'"

Humorists are alive and creative in their perceptions. To develop your ability to expand the horrible, try a few exercises to deal with approval, perfection, or fear of making a decision. Jot down your responses.

Exercise 1

A. What is the worst thing that could happen if someone who I really want to like me doesn't? (Don't limit yourself to time or space.)

B. What would I do if this happened?

Exercise 2

A. What is the worst mistake I could conceive of making?

B. What would I do if this happened?

Exercise 3

A. What is the toughest decision I could be forced to make? What would be the worst possible consequence of making a bad decision?

B. What would I do if I made the bad decision?

Humor And Negative Emotions

The creative humorist looks for new ways of understanding the concerns of people. For example, humorists may describe negative and immobilizing emotions as a "vacation." Here are a few exercises that might be used with a person who is experiencing guilt, anger, or depression.

Exercise 1. Your negative emotions are like a vacation. When you are experiencing guilt about a past event, you are retreating to your yacht. Your yacht is located on the Sea of Fantasy off the coast of Reality. As you peer out the window from the lounge, what are all the things you can tell yourself about your failures and lack of self-worth? How is it easier, and in fact a vacation, to spend your time feeling guilty rather than acting differently?

Exercise 2. Creatively develop a travel brochure to show all the benefits involved in thinking about the past.

Exercise 3. Show the power of your depression on the lives of those around you.

Develop five good reasons why you should become **depressed** when things don't go your way:

1.

2.

3.

4.

5.

Exercise 4. You are in a courtroom representing the positive effects of whining or getting your own way. Present your argument.

Exercise 5. Demonstrate how the use of creative blaming can keep you from facing the "horrible" realities of life.

1.   Blame self (i.e., *I am horrible*):

2.   Blame other people (i.e., *my mother-in-law*):

3.   Blame other groups (i.e., *the Russians*):

4.   Blame the world (i.e., *this traffic drives me up a wall*):

Develop some creative exercises of your own to increase your skill in using humor.

Reducing Interpersonal Conflict Through Humor

Discouraged people have limited vision and believe they are seeing "what is" in the only possible correct way. They face the ultimate *paradox* when they conclude that "the person with whom I disagree the most has a viewpoint that makes as much sense to him or her as my viewpoint does to me." How can this be resolved? One way is to say, "I'm right and you're wrong." But this does not accept the other person's point of view. This also gives the other person the logical right to not accept my point of view. Thus, the conflict continues. Humorists help to expand the phenomenology of the parties in conflict, to broaden their points of view. The following exercises can help to expand your perceptions.

Exercise 1. Try to "be the other as best you can." Imagine you look exactly like the other party in a disagreement and have had all their experiences of life. Present the argument of the other side as vigorously as you would present your own side.

Exercise 2. Now be a mediator. Stand above both you and the other party, with absolutely no loyalty to either, and objectively try to decide the half-way point in their argument.

Exercise 3. Think of a controversial issue about which you have strong feelings in one direction. Now get into the world of the other side and see it through their eyes. Present the other's case with the same energy that you would have presented yours.

Exercise 4. Humorously show yourself how narrow-minded you previously were on this issue.

Yes, life is an unlimited series of interesting paradoxes. It is through their ability to switch perspectives that humorists enable discouraged people to expand their vision. This is true encouragement. As O'Connell (1969) wrote, "Humor is a rare product of the effort to see with the eyes and hear with the ears of another, across time and space, using positive sense rather than negative nonsense."

Application Of Responding With Humor

Situation 1. "I just couldn't stand it if Steve didn't like my new dress. That would be devastating."
Your response:

Situation 2.   You are taking a friend to an athletic event. When you arrive at the stadium, there is no one around. You look at your tickets and realize you are there on the wrong day.
   Your response:

References

Dinkmeyer, Don. *The Basics of Self-Acceptance.* Coral Springs, FL: CMTI Press, 1992.

Greenberg, D. and Jacobs, M. *How to Make Yourself Miserable.* NY: Random House, 1966.

O'Connell, Walter. Humor: The Therapeutic Impasse. *Voices: The Art and Science of Psychotherapy.* 5(1909):25–27, 1969.

O'Connell, Walter. Personal communication, 1995.

12

Recognizing Discouraging Belief Skills

Wh-hen we are discouraged, it is not because of the way things are; it is because of the way we are looking at things. When we change our beliefs about a situation, we change our discouragement into either acceptance or courage.

Diane has the ability to get us thinking about things in a new way when we are discouraged. "You didn't fail, you learned something here didn't you? If you wouldn't have tried, you would not have known what you know now. You have never been more knowledgeable than you are at this moment because of what you learned," your encourager proclaims. Diane enlightens and lightens you at tough times with beliefs like, "Backing your car into the pole isn't a tragedy. It's a minor inconvenience." Diane would make an insightful counselor, social worker, or parent because of her ability to add new dimensions to the way others think about things.

Diane has the skills to recognize a person's discouraging beliefs. In this chapter, you will develop the skills to turn any discouraged person's mind around and begin looking up rather than down, forward rather than backward.

Joanna is frustrated and bitter about the "raw deal" that she believes she received in life. She feels that her older sister is much more attractive than she and her younger brother is their parents' favorite.

She constantly complains about all the unfair things that have happened to her. She believes life is unfair.

Kevin believes that the worst thing that could happen to him would be to make a mistake. He needs to be perfect in everything. If he does make an error, he relives the mistake over and over again. His life has become a safe routine, and he never takes any chances. Kevin feels that in this way, he need not fear failing. If he does not try, he cannot fail. He believes mistakes are dangerous.

Joanna and Kevin are just two examples of how negative beliefs can discourage people from living the full odyssey of their lives. Joanna may live out her 30,000 days with a handicap—the belief that the world *must* be fair. As long as she continues to tell herself this discouraging thought, it will continue to affect the way she sees the events in her life. Because of Joanna's outlook, can you imagine how unrewarding it is for people to be around her?

Did you ever know someone like Joanna, who constantly complained about injustice? Perhaps you decided to stay away from this person, because he or she became a discouraging influence on you. Unfortunately, when people stay away, the vicious cycle continues. Joanna sees this rejection as further proof that the world is unfair, for she, unlike her siblings, has no friends. What she fails to realize is that she has played the major role in determining this rejection.

Kevin has come to believe that unless he is perfect in everything that he does, he is worthless. There is no such thing as a B grade for Kevin. Anything less than an A is a failure in his book. The safest way for Kevin to protect his self-esteem is not to try. By not trying, he cannot fail.

This chapter illustrates how to identify the discouraging beliefs that people like Joanna and Kevin have toward themselves, others, and their lives. For example, as long as Joanna believes that the world *must* be fair, we can predict that her life will be full of disappointments, frustrations, and anger. Kevin's belief that he *must* be perfect in everything he does will dictate that his one lifetime of possibilities is constricted. He will limit his world only to what he knows he can do well. After identifying some discouraging beliefs, we will discuss ways of helping such people overcome their constrictions and thus open up new hopes and goals for them.

Challenging Discouraging Beliefs: Where Does It Fit In As A Skill?

The skills discussed so far will help you to build positive and encouraging relationships. Through your use of communication skills, agreement, believing, enthusiasm, and various methods of focusing, you have invited people to feel heard, trusted, and significant in their relationships with you. If the positive person possesses high levels of empathy, warmth, and respect, these are sufficient for growth to occur. While this may be enough in some cases, the more additional skills the helper has, the more likely he or she is to foster encouragement.

Empathy helps the encourager to more effectively understand feelings and emotions. Understanding feelings provides the encourager with clues about the way people look at life. Consider again Joanna and Kevin. It was through first understanding Joanna's emotions—anger and disappointment—that we were directed to the source of her perceptions about her life. We also observed Kevin's anxiety about failure or imperfections. These emotions gave us indications about his discouraging beliefs.

Empathy, then, helps us to understand emotions. Emotions are servants to the beliefs of people. Whenever we see crippling emotions, our encouraging antennas are extended to identify the beliefs to which people's constrictions are turned. It is by altering faulty perceptions that a whole new life, including emotions and behavior, can occur. Encouragement, then, is perception modification.

In *You Can Do It* (1980), Losoncy suggested that encouragement involves inviting people to correct two basic mistakes in the way they look at life. He wrote:

> Much discouragement is the result of two basic mistaken beliefs about self, others, and life. The first error is in the failure of people to face and accept reality as it is. The second major mistake is in the failure of people to realize all of the possible alternatives still available to them once they face and accept that reality.
>
> Discouragement occurs when people fail to overcome one or both of these errors. The unwillingness of people to

accept reality as it is results from a superiority complex. They place themselves out of perspective in the universe, believing that the world has focused in on them personally. This, of course, is naive and self-defeating and results in the feelings of grandiosity and persecution as is often seen in the paranoid person.

The second mistake that hinders human happiness is the unwillingness of people to realize all of the possible alternatives still available to them once they face and accept that reality. When people make this mistake, they become overwhelmed by the universal reality, giving it too much credit and blame. These people are unaware of their life possibilities and feel hopeless and helpless. They are passive victims to what they see as the powerful forces of life and other people.

Either mistake of underplaying or overplaying the importance of reality results in discouragement. The process of overcoming both of these discouraging beliefs is perhaps the most important road to the courageous life. Yet, it is perhaps the most complicated task of life because many of us continue to go on making error #1, disrespecting reality, or error #2, disrespecting ourselves.

Encouraging people invite people to face and accept those things in their lives that they choose not to change and help them to develop perceptual alternatives within that reality. Also, at the appropriate time in an encouraging relationship, as determined by the encourager's judgment of helpee readiness, providing feedback about faulty beliefs can help to develop courage.

Skills In Identifying Some Discouraging Beliefs

As a positive person, become aware of the following and other faulty beliefs and learn to associate them with certain emotional complaints.

Need For Approval As A Discouraging Belief

"I am only okay when people give me their stamp of approval. When they disapprove of me or even when they say nothing, I become more worthless and *must* feel hurt or angry."

Lee is interested in becoming a teacher, but his parents, both medical doctors, are pushing him to follow in their footsteps. Lee feels pressured to become a doctor, despite his internal pull toward teaching. He fears that his parents will disapprove of him unless he follows their direction.

Carmen, a college sophomore, enjoys a certain professor whom her classmates dislike. The students draw up a petition to have the professor removed because he is too demanding. This doesn't make sense to Carmen, since she believes she has learned a great deal from this professor. But when her classmates approach her, she cooperatively signs the petition.

Have you, like Lee and Carmen, ever done something because you believed it was what someone else wanted, instead of what you wanted? Do you ever say something just because you believe it is what others want to hear, rather than what you believe? Do you avoid speaking out when you disagree because you believe your opinions are not as worthwhile as the ideas of others? Perhaps you, in these moments, are regulated by the approval of others.

Humans, out of their childhood need to be taken care of, strive to be liked and approved of. This is healthy in the sense that children need other people to help take care of their needs for food, warmth, and safety. As long as people have not developed the skills to survive independently, it is logical that they need others.

With increasing maturity and mastery over their environment, children become more self-reliant. As they enter school, they learn that they are no longer the center of the universe and will not be constantly served by others. They must share the limelight with many others. They learn that they are expected to contribute and that they can give as well as take. They also, one hopes, learn that they have opinions, beliefs, and ideas of their own that count.

When people are invited to develop their own beliefs and are accepted regardless of whether their ideas conform to those of the individual who holds the stamp of approval, self-trust begins. With self-trust comes courage. People with this self-trust are referred to as an "internal locus of evaluation." "Internal trusters" have values that are based upon what *they* believe, as opposed to "external trusters," whose values are determined by others. People who evaluate internally are open to the opinions of others but, in the end, take full responsibility for the beliefs and decisions in their lives. While they *want* the approval of other, they do not *need* it.

What does the difference between *wanting approval* and *needing approval* mean to you?

List some comments or actions which would indicate that the helpee is a victim of the fictitious need for approval. For example, "I couldn't stand it if my boss didn't like my ideas."

Need For Perfection As A Discouraging Belief

"I'm only okay when I do things perfectly. If I make a mistake, show a flaw or an imperfection, or even fail at something, I become worthless and will remain so for the rest of my days."

Jennifer believes that unless she looks perfect, she should not go out. Before she goes to a party, she works on herself for hours, making sure that every detail is flawless. Sometimes Jennifer does not even go out because she fails to fulfill her dire need for super-humanness.

Nine-year-old Freddie hates art class. When his teacher asks the class to draw, Freddie defensively covers his paper with his arms, shoulders, and head and proceeds to draw at what seems to be a pace of one inch per hour! Vast amounts of Freddie's time and energies are spent erasing in frustration because his elephant is not perfect. Interestingly, Freddie always seems to have a stomach ache on Friday afternoons. Care to guess the day when his art class takes place?

Clues about the need for perfection are evidenced in emotions and behavior. By observing that Jennifer will take hours to prepare herself or will panic if she sees a wrinkle, you as a helper can become aware of her stifling *need*. Freddie's defensive behavior and stomach aches may be tip-offs to his thoughts that "I *must* be perfect in art."

Both Jennifer and Freddie, similar to many other people with perfection needs (for example, Kevin in our earlier illustration), constrict their lives within narrow but safe boundaries. This need for perfection is so all-encompassing that a good criterion for the effectiveness of encouragement is to observe whether helpers take risks and try new experiences. Rudolf Dreikurs, in his now-famous quotation, referred to the courageous person as one who has the "courage to be imperfect." Think about this quotation for a few seconds; then jot down what it means to you. Dreikurs suggested that the more discouraged a person is, the more a person seeks and needs perfection. Are there areas in your life where you have the courage to be imperfect, where it doesn't bother you to make a mistake? Are there other areas where a mistake is devastating to you? If so, why the difference?

When people have the courage to be imperfect, their possibilities in life become unlimited. Nothing becomes unreachable.

You can recognize perfection needs by any of the following feelings or behaviors:

1. Immobilization or inaction

2. Ego-involvement as opposed to task-involvement

For example:

Ego-Involvement	Task-Involvement
Must have own way	Looks for the best way; if someone else's way is more effective, then that way is more appropriate
Closed-minded	Open-minded
Panics when wrong	Learns from errors to improve future behaviors

Perfection needs can also be recognized by the following feelings or behaviors:

3. Constant planning rather than doing

4. Blaming others, the world, or circumstances for errors

5. Never relaxed, always on guard

6. Highly critical or others' mistakes

7. Stereotyped behavior, predictable most days, a routine

8. Traumatic behavior change

9. Panicking when things and people do not fit into place

10. Seeing the world and people in clear-cut, black-and-white ways

Add some other behaviors that you have observed in the person with perfection needs.

Need For Irresponsibility, Or Blaming, As A Discouraging Belief

"I am not responsible for my life. What made me the way I am today were things like my parents, my friends, my teachers, and other factors in my environment and in my genes. I cannot change until things and powerful forces outside of me change first."

Michael explains that his fear of women was caused by his weak father and domineering mother, who gave him the impression that women were strong and to be feared and that men were powerless. He says that there is nothing he can do to offset such devastating environmental experiences, and thus unhappily but safely continues his self-defeating inaction. He believes, "I am not responsible for myself."

Jeff says that he never finished college because he could not possibly pass the required math course. He says, "You see, I am the kind of person who cannot do math, and so I decided to quit college. But that's not surprising, considering that no one in my family was good at math either."

Both Michael and Jeff feel helpless and not responsible for their feelings, thoughts, and actions. Michael's early environmental conditioning is his excuse to live his life unfulfilled. Jeff perhaps believes that he is doomed not to be a college graduate because of a deficiency in math.

Although it might be difficult for both Michael and Jeff to overcome some of their discouragement, with determination it is possible. We might even ask Jeff, "Do you mean that if you put all your energies toward mastering math by (1) hiring an effective private tutor and (2) buying the best and simplest math books available, in a matter of a few weeks would you not know more about math than you do now?"

The problem with overcoming feelings of helplessness is that there are many fringe benefits to claiming irresponsibility. Can you think of how having these feelings of being powerless might give a person permission not to succeed? Give some examples.

Identify some feelings, thoughts, or actions you might observe which demonstrate that people suffer from the fiction of irresponsibility. For example, "I just couldn't tell my boss that she is making me angry," or "I could never tell people how I honestly feel about them."

Once you have identified a stifling belief, you can invite the discouraged person to attack and remove the faulty vision and thus lead to a fuller life.

Application Of Recognizing Discouraging Belief Skills

Respond to the following statements by identifying discouraging beliefs.

Statement 1. "I can't hold a job. That's because both my parents worked when I was young and they weren't there to push me to develop mature behaviors."
  List a discouraging belief and explain your choice:

Statement 2. "I don't understand it. I even bought a new car to help my popularity at school, but still no one seems to care about bothering with me. I constantly go out of my way for others and it just doesn't help. I can't take it anymore."
  List a discouraging belief and explain your choice:

Statement 3. "I'm so frustrated. I bought this new tie to go with my new suit for tonight's party but it doesn't quite match, and I have no other tie that will match. I'm thinking about not going."

List a discouraging belief and explain your choice:

Answers:

1. Irresponsibility or blaming fiction

2. Approval fiction

3. Perfection fiction

References

Dreikurs, Rudolf. Dreikurs Sayings. *The Individual Psychologist*. Vol. IX No. 2, November 1972.

Losoncy, Lewis. *You Can Do It*. New York: Simon & Schuster, 1980.

13

Focusing On Effort Skills

Scott focuses intensively on seeing any progress or movement. He notices progress that may be imperceptible to most of us. If he notices any slight movement, he comments in a positive way.

Scott teaches tennis and has found this skill to be a great resource in his work. He is able to notice a slightly greater agility in moving about the court or getting in position to use a certain stroke. He does not expect perfect strokes, perfect footwork, or perfect focus. Instead, he takes every opportunity available to support, encourage, and focus on the efforts and attempts his students make.

He has learned to transfer this skill to his relationship with his family. His daughter plays a musical instrument. When she practices and plays some of the notes correctly and others incorrectly, he comments on the correct notes. When his son brings home a spelling paper with some of the words right and others wrong, he talks first about the words that are spelled right.

Scott has learned to focus on the effort rather than perfect results. By focusing on effort, you will find improvement in your relationships and, even more important, improvement in the skills of the individuals with whom you are working.

We live in a culture that expects us to do our very best. As the saying goes, anything worth doing is worth doing well. However, if we think about it, there are a number of things worth doing as well as we can without any expectation that they be perfect. One of the major limitations to our satisfaction is the emphasis on complete and outstanding results. If we only do the things we do well, we limit our possibilities for enjoyment. Take athletic skills as an example. If only the bowlers who were able to throw a 300 game bowled or if only the golfers who shot very close to par golfed, there would be a lot of people who would not be able to enjoy these games as a hobby. Obviously, this would also apply to dancing, swimming, and a variety of other activities.

Focusing on efforts and contributions contrasts with focusing only on completed actions or outstanding behaviors. For example, your son Jimmy, age eight, brings home a school math paper on which he has gotten three right and seventeen wrong. The teacher has clearly marked the paper "fail" and was not interested in Jimmy's efforts. When Jimmy hands you his paper, you have a choice about how you will respond. You can respond to either the seventeen wrong or the three right. If you respond to the three right, you show creative, spontaneous behavior. In responding to the three problems that are correct, you have an opportunity to increase Jimmy's self-esteem, motivation, and interest in math. You might say, "You seemed to do very well on the addition problems. I can see you started out very well. Your answers on subtraction are usually close to the correct answer. Would you like to practice subtraction?" This communicates that you are not shocked or overly disturbed by the poor paper. You don't see it as a personal problem. At the same time, you are able to see a lot of positive things in Jimmy's work and you have decided to support him. Your focus on effort does not attack or assassinate character.

Your husband has been anticipating a raise in his paycheck. Today is payday and you can tell from his face that things did not go well. He says, "Well, they raised me ten dollars a week, or two dollars a day. I might as well be delivering newspapers. I'd get a bigger raise than this." You can begin by responding empathically by saying, "You're really disappointed" or "It doesn't seem fair." Then, you can look for ways to recognize his effort. If you are familiar with his job, you can comment on something he has been recognized for, like "They were really enthusiastic about that new account you brought in." You focus away from the disappointment of the paycheck to recognize an effort or contribution. "It looks like you put all your concern into what the company thinks of you financially, right now. Is that why your raise is so disappointing?" If the answer is affirmative, you have a chance to discuss how you can't always force things to happen. Then, give some thought to ways your spouse is progressing in the company (types of assignments, recognition, or involvement in decision making). Help your spouse move forward, even if his contribution is not being recognized financially at this time.

When you focus on effort, you are taking a different perceptual approach to the situation. You are not burdened by the limitations, the negative occurrences, or anything else that appears to restrict the individual's progress. Instead, you focus on strengths, assets, or anything that shows positive movement. You clearly focus on the effort instead of only the final product. This emphasis on the effort provides a unique way of supporting the individual who is still in the process of moving toward greater success.

Perceptual alternative skills are helpful in the process of focusing on efforts. These alternatives help you recognize any positive effort the person is making, even though not directly in the area of criticism or concern. You can recognize improved physical fitness, developing new skills, participating in new activities, spiritual development, and new and rewarding relationships with friends or children.

One of the problems in focusing on effort is the way in which we are constricted and restricted by our tunnel vision. We become trapped by the importance we put on certain aspects of life. For example, by focusing on financial gains and rewards, you may become totally discouraged if the bottom line is that your company will not pay any more at this time. This is when you have to keep your vistas open to the total range of events occurring in your life and see what is possible for you and where you can make efforts that will be rewarding to you.

You and Tom, a friend, are playing doubles in the local tennis tournament. You have both improved a lot but have just lost to a team that you both know you could have beaten. During the match, your opponents regularly directed the ball to Tom at the net. He seldom was able to return the ball, and as the match continued, it became evident that they were going to hit as many balls as possible to Tom. After the match, Tom says, "Well, I really blew that match. I had four lessons this month and came out for extra practice, but it was a waste of time. I think I'm going to give up tennis. I'm sure you can find a partner who won't be such a handicap."

You might focus on Tom's efforts and say, "You really improved your backhand and played a steady game," or "I liked the way you kept battling even when we were behind," or "Your lobs and volleys made it possible for me to look good on the put-away shots."

The encouraging person finds a way to recognize something of value even when others have given up. It is always possible to focus on another person's efforts, attempts, or any positive movement. For example, it is especially encouraging for people to be able to note, "Last month you were only able to walk a mile in [a certain period of time]. You are now five seconds faster," or "I see your golf score last year averaged 110 and now you are down to 104." These are both opportunities to recognize effort, which enables a person to continue to move forward.

Movement is the essence of success. It indicates that you are headed toward a goal, and any movement toward a goal is progress. It is essential to recognize that any simple steps in the right direction merit recognition. If a young child who was just beginning to walk struggled to stand up, took one step, and fell down, you certainly wouldn't say, "Don't try that again until you can do it right and take ten steps at once." Instead, you observe any effort, movement, or progress.

The person who makes an initial effort needs to be encouraged, because encouragement supplies the support to sustain the effort that has begun but may be faltering. Sometimes, a few simple words which recognize the effort being made are all that is needed to sustain the effort.

At this time, it is equally important to recognize that when you are trying to shift to a more encouraging way of life, you, too, need to be self-encouraging. This includes recognizing your progress in encouragement and not merely identifying your faults. For example, be aware of your growing consciousness of the opportunities to encourage. You may have formerly greeted people with, "How are you?" Now you say, "You're looking good. I like your outfit. I noticed how well you seem to be doing." Maybe at one time it was difficult for you to accept people who are different from you and you didn't even try to encourage them. Now you consciously seek to greet them. Maybe you thought that life was competitive and only a victory was praiseworthy. Now you are able to encourage someone who makes an attempt to contribute in a unique way even thought it may not be noteworthy.

Opportunities to encourage include setting the table, preparing food, going to the store, cutting the law, running an errand—the list is endless.

As you focus on the efforts of others, you become aware of the many opportunities to encourage. You realize how subtle and small some of these efforts are. You may be surprised at the results of recognizing and encouraging small efforts. It will open up a whole new vista to positive relationships.

Let's see whether you can focus on efforts and contributions in the following situations.

Situation 1.   Your child is helping you set the table. He has put silverware at all the place settings but the forks and knives are reversed. He has just finished and stands next to the table beaming, with a smile from ear to ear.

What do you say? What do you do?

Situation 2.   You are in the second week of your diet. Your neighbor comes over and says, "Have I got a surprise for you!" as she uncovers a cake she has baked for you.

What do you say? What do you do?

Situation 3. Your new secretary is very effective on the telephone but has problems with dictation and typing. She brings you an important letter with a number of typographical errors.
What do you say? What do you do?

Situation 4. Your husband rarely goes shopping for you. He usually gives you money so you can buy something you like. Today he brings you an attractive blouse two sizes too large.
What do you say? What do you do?

It must be stressed that your ability to see potential strengths and good intentions has a great deal to do with your ability as an encourager.

The athlete who works extra hard and completes a ten-mile race, even though finishing near the end of the competition, has made an effort. The person who weighs 210 pounds and loses 6 pounds has made an effort. The student who failed all courses the first term and now is passing two of five courses is making an effort.

None of the above-mentioned efforts are outstanding, nor are they something that most people would consider noteworthy. However, the effort can be noteworthy in the eyes of the person who recognizes the movement that has occurred. This encouragement can become a source of motivation and can positively affect a person's self-worth.

Our society recognizes the outstanding athlete, the well-known actor, and famous newsmaker. However, recognition is not given for trying or contributing. You may know the names of Dan Marino and Joe Montana, excellent professional football quarterbacks, but do you know the names of the linesmen who made it possible for them to succeed? You may be acquainted with the giants of business, industry, and finance, but do you know the names of their advisers?

You may not think you are outstanding, but you are making a

uniquely valuable contribution through your ability to perceive effort and influence others.

How would you respond to effort in the following situations?

Situation 1.   Your four-year-old child has just brought you a drawing she has spent a lot of time on. It looks like a disorganized and confusing scribble.
> *What do you say? What do you do?*

Situation 2.   You are a coach of a Little League baseball team. The team tried very hard in an important game, made some good catches and hits, but lost. They appear to be very discouraged.
> *What do you say? What do you do?*

Situation 3.   Your child has spent a long time cutting the lawn but missed a large area next to the garage.
> *What do you say? What do you do?*

Situation 4.   An employee in your shoe store goes back to the stock room and climbs to the top of the ladder to find the size he thinks you need. When he hands you the box, you notice that the shoes are a half size too small.
> *What do you say? What do you do?*

Situation 5.   Your spouse tries to help with the cooking but burns the meat.
> *What do you say? What do you do?*

You may have attained high points in your life, times when you were at your very best. These times may have gone unnoticed by the rest of the world, but for you they were satisfying.

Here are some events that some people considered to be their high points:

- Billy, age five, can swim one length of the pool.

- Janet, age seven, is the best tumbler in her class at school.

- Fred never fails to associate a name with a face.

- You balanced your checkbook.

- Pam has just started a catering business and is asked to bake the wedding cake for a friend's wedding.

- Shirley discovers new, appetizing ideas for her children's lunches.

- Larry, who works in the mail room, is able to guess the weight of a package to within an ounce.

What are some of your high points?

Too often, evaluations and worth are based on money, prestige, or an outstanding talent. For example, the wealthy may get special seating privileges in theaters or restaurants. Stars of entertainment or athletics may be given special services. Even in school, students with the most obvious talent may get more recognition. Unfortunately, this type of thinking blinds us from seeing the potential of the average person.

Encouragers identify interests and translate them into assets. Think of a discouraged person you know, someone who is not sure of himself or herself and is not self-confident. Think of some areas (intellectual, musical, athletic, social, nurturing, mechanical) where this person has talents, assets, or potential high points. Remember, instead of an outstanding ability, you are looking for something that is personally satisfying and rewarding to the individual.

Encouragers really value human life. They see something good in each person and are eager to highlight that asset, strength, or effort. Encouragers see how the incomplete can become complete, enjoy lifting people up, look for what is good, and ignore what is bad. They recognize that they can only help people grow by focusing on what is positive. They can always find a way to help a person move away from discouragement. Encouragers are talented at seeing positive potential and commenting on it.

An encourager focuses on:

1. Attempts

2. Tries

3. Any movement

4. Beginnings

5. Observing struggles and supporting the person who moves toward progress

6. Recognizing intentions

Application Of Focusing On Efforts And Contributions

Situation 1. *Eleanor:* "I was so determined to cut my calorie intake from 2000 to 1500. But I haven't succeeded yet. I averaged 1800 calories over the past week. I doubt that I will ever make it."
Your response:

Situation 2. Your five-year-old son is playing baseball at a family picnic. He hits the ball, but instead of running to first base, he runs to third base. Everyone starts yelling at him.
Your response:

Situation 3.   You are a supervisor. One of your workers gives you a suggestion for how to make things better at your company. The suggestion strikes you as absurd.

   Your response:

_____

14 Rational Thinking Skills To Defeat Discouragement

Rachel has a way of bringing us back to reality and adding common sense to our lives. When we complain that it shouldn't be raining because we planned a picnic, Rachel quickly points out that it should be raining because it is raining. She says, "It isn't raining to keep us from going on our picnic. It's raining because the atmospheric conditions are right for rain!"

Rachel helps us to change our belief from "All events in the world must go my way" to "While I would like everything in the universe to go my way, it doesn't have to. I can stand it when things don't go my way." Rachel moves us from our discouraging irrational, grandiose thoughts of "I must be perfect in everything I do every day for the rest of my life" to the more rational belief that "I would like to be perfect, but I don't need to be perfect. Let me do my best." Rachel would be close to perfect as a teacher, counselor, psychologist, or parent because of her ability to add common sense to a person's life.

Rachel has rational thinking skills. In this chapter, you will acquire the skills to reasonably change your own life, as well as the lives of those around you.

You no doubt have heard the phrase you are what you eat. Medical researchers find more evidence each day to support the belief that the food you eat has a powerful impact on you. If you are like most people, you find that a well-balanced diet gives you increased energy and better feelings about yourself, as well as approval from your doctor at checkup time.

Yes, you are what you eat. This is exciting and powerful news. Why? Because it tells you that you have control over a very important aspect of your life: your physical well-being. Just by becoming the master of your diet, you have the freedom to select foods that will make you happier and healthier (assuming, of course, that you can say no to people who are trying to force you to eat something that will make you sluggish and plump).

Few people would disagree that you are what you eat. And just as you are what you eat, **you are what you think**. The most powerful psychological revelation of the decade is the realization that your thinking creates not only your emotions but also your actions. Behavioral research and clinical experience accumulate more evidence each day to show the relationships between your thinking and (1) your depression, (2) your anxieties, (3) your fears, (4) your guilt, (5) your temper and other anger-related problems, (6) your feelings of failure and inferiority, and (7) your overall unhappiness and dissatisfaction in life.

The implications of your thinking do not stop with these seven emotional problems. Research also supports the belief that your thinking even plays a major role in psychosomatic disorders such as (1) ulcers, (2) migraine headaches, (3) hypertension, and (4) some forms of obesity. Not only does your thinking create symptoms and unhappiness, but your thoughts are the source of positive emotions and happiness. You definitely are what you think!

The great news is that, just as you can be the master of your diet, you can be the master of your thoughts. You can be healthier and happier and better able to make your feelings and actions work for you. Imagine the enormous human power you have when you become master of both your physical and psychological selves through a well-balanced diet and through rational thinking.

This chapter focuses on how you can rid yourself of emotional problems and win success and happiness by using the powerful artillery of rational thinking, the greatest human weapon against unhappiness. While the power of rational thinking has only recently been scientifically demonstrated, it has been advocated for over twenty centuries.

Belief In Rational Thinking: Not New But Scientifically True

Humanity has always been cognizant of the power present in the way a person looks at things. Over 2000 years ago, the Stoic philosopher Epictetus argued, "No human is free who is not master of his or her thoughts." Either we are masters of our thoughts (rational thinking) or we are helpless slaves to our thoughts (irrational thinking). Epictetus concluded, "Humans are not disturbed by things, but by the views which they take of them." A red light, a traffic jam, and rainy weather are not negative events in themselves. Actually, they are neutral. These events cannot cause our emotions, unhappiness, disturbance, or an ulcer. However, the things that happen to you take on meaning the very second that you give the neutral events in your life a positive or a negative meaning. You can choose to say, "This red light makes me angry," or "I'm glad I got stopped at this red light. Now I can check the map of the city," or even, "So what if the light is red? I'll only have to stop for a few seconds." It is your view of the situation, and not the color of the light, that causes the emotional tension or personal frustration. The light is neither good nor bad in itself; it just is.

Epictetus, an early rational thinker, was suggesting that we, as human beings, have the option of choosing how to view what happens to us in our lives. Can you remember the last time you allowed a neutral event to be your master and create depression, anger, or unhappiness?

A few years following the time of Epictetus, the Roman Emperor Marcus Aurelius echoed the assertions of the early Stoic by writing, "No human is happy who does not make himself or herself so." Success and happiness are won, and they can be won by everyone regardless of what life sends their way if they use rational thinking.

Immanuel Kant, the 18th century philosopher, exalted the power of the way things are perceived. Kant divided human experience into two areas: (1) *noumena,* or the things that are "out there" (e.g., the rainy weather, the high price of meat, the economy, etc.) and (2) *phenomena,* or the things that you perceive from the noumena (e.g., this weather makes me miserable, the high price of meat is unfair, the economy has gone down the drain, etc.). Kant proclaimed that to truly understand people, we need to look not at the noumena but at the phenomena. That is, ten people could experience the same noumena, the same life experience, but they would have ten different reactions to it. In the end, it is the way that you think about an experience that affects you.

Psychiatrist Alfred Adler, in our opinion the greatest practical thinker of the century, wrote about the creative power your thoughts have to overcome barriers:

> Do not forget the most important fact that neither heredity nor environment are determining factors. Both are giving only the frame and the influences which are answered by the individual in regard to his styled creative self.
>
> Ansbacher and Ansbacher, 1956

What happens to us in life does not affect us. The view we take of events does.

Victor Frankl, in his book *Man's Search for Meaning* (1959), wrote about his experience of being imprisoned in a war camp with apparently little chance of survival. The author described how the prison guards stripped him, barely fed him, and dehumanized him. Frankl concluded that the guards could do anything they wanted to do to him, and he was helpless to stop them. But the one thing they couldn't do to him was affect the way he chose to look at his life. And, in the end, the way we view our life is what really counts. Frankl's powerful outlook gave him a strong will and kept him going, which proves that the power of rational thinking can make a person the master of any life experience.

Moorhead Kennedy, a U.S. hostage in Iran, faced death many times during his 444 days in captivity. He was awakened in the middle of many nights and told that he would be shot in the next few minutes. Each day it was a challenge just to make it to bed alive, where he wondered if he would ever see the sun again. Despite the continuous strain that he experienced, Kennedy proclaimed, "We have been through one of the toughest experiences a human could go through, and we survived pretty darn well." He went on to conclude that a great deal of good came out of a bad situation. The ex-hostage proudly asserted, "Our experiences brought the American people together, and few experiences in our lifetime could have done that." Kennedy demonstrated the power of the view you take toward what happens to you in life.

A pearl begins as an irritating grain of sand and develops into a gem. Pearls are obstacles that become opportunities. When you use the power of rational thinking, like Frankl and Kennedy, you might create a string of pearls in your lifetime!

We have seen the power that outlook has given human beings from the days of Epictetus up to the present time. But only recently has rational thinking been developed systematically so that everyone can use the same strength that Frankl, Kennedy, and most successful people use. The credit for this unparalleled discovery of rational thinking goes to Drs. Albert Ellis and Robert Harper. In *A New Guide to Rational Living*, the book most recommended by psychologists, the authors wrote:

> When we first began thinking and writing about rational emotive therapy in the latter half of the 1950's, we could cite little research material to back up the idea that humans do not get upset, but that they upset themselves by devoutly convincing themselves of irrational beliefs about what happens to them. Since that time hundreds of experiments have clearly demonstrated that if an experimenter induces, by fair or foul means, individuals to change their thoughts, they also profoundly change their emotions and behavior.
>
> Ellis and Harper, 1975

Research confirms this point. You can lead a successful and happy life by using one of the greatest gifts you have—the power of rational thinking.

Rational Thinking: Your Thoughts Control Your Emotions And Actions

Your emotions, whether positive or negative, are a result of your thinking. Your actions, whether successful or unsuccessful, are also products of your thoughts. Consider a person who claims to have an inferiority complex. Feelings of inferiority and actions that tell of inferiority develop the second a person thinks of himself or herself as inferior. And a person's feelings of inferiority will predictably continue for as long as this person concludes "I am inferior." But those same feelings of inferiority cease the day, the hour, the minute, the very second that the person begins to see himself or herself in a new and more rational way. Consider the following way of understanding human thoughts, feelings, and behavior:

Thinking or Believing	Creates	Feelings or Emotions	Which in Turn Creates	Behavior or Actions
Irrational statement				
"I am an inferior person." (unprovable and thus irrational)		"I'm so unhappy. I'm worthless and can't do anything right. I feel horrible. I'm so inadequate."		This person doesn't take chances and gives up because of not trying or not developing skills.

The moment a person concludes "I am an inferior person," an inferiority complex is born. This person's emotions, actions, or inactions dance to the tune of his or her beliefs, and his or her unhappiness and failure to act are a result of an irrational belief that he or she is inferior. The key point of this chapter is how you can use these colossal powers of rational thinking in your everyday life to achieve success and happiness.

Rational Versus Irrational Thinking: Know The Difference, Feel The Difference, Live The Difference

What is irrational? Why is believing "I am an inferior person" not provable and, as a result, irrational? The statement is an over-generalization and is not a fact. Remember, however, that even though it isn't a fact, it still has a powerful effect on the person who treats it as a fact. Why isn't the comment a fact? The answer is that no one can possibly be an inferior person. There is no scale on which to measure the total person or conclude that one human being is inferior to another. There is no proof, and thus the belief is invalid and irrational.

Now observe how we could produce a more rational and thus a more productive way of thinking. Remember, a rational statement is one that can be proven. I could say, "I am an *inferior skier* to the world's top skier." I could even say, "I am the worst skier in the whole world" or "Every single person in the world is a superior skier to me." Suppose that somehow I could, in fact, prove that every single person in the world is a more talented skier than I am. This would make me an *inferior skier* (quite rational and provable), but it would not make me an *inferior person* (irrational and unprovable.) Besides, I can dance better than some people, I can sing better than some people, I can spell better than some people, etc., if, of course, I make comparisons important to me.

Observe how rational beliefs create rational feelings and actions.

Rational Beliefs or Behaviors	Create	Rational Feelings or Thoughts	Which In Turn Create	Rational Thoughts or Actions
(Provable and thus rational)		(Enjoyment, happiness)		(Heading toward success)
"I am inferior at skiing to many other people."		"Because my total expertise and capabilities do not depend on just my ability to ski, I can enjoy myself and learn new skiing techniques without the fear of failure."		This person skis and finds it enjoyable because the tensions were removed. This person practices more frequently and actually improves his or her skiing ability.

Be A Rational Thinker: It's As Easy As A-B-C

How can you make use of the systematic process of rational thinking to help you achieve success and happiness? You can start by learning the A-B-C's of rational thinking. Take a few minutes to memorize the following statements, and soon you will have the opportunity to put the system to use.

Rational Thinking

Let's deal with A and C first:

Activating event or experience in your life

Consequent emotion that you experience after the event

Do you believe that events in your life cause your emotions? If so, (A) when something happens to you (e.g., failing a test), (C) you experience the consequent emotion of perhaps depression as a result of the event. This could be viewed as A causes C. Is this formula true? Suppose you fail an exam, which becomes an activating event (A) to cause your consequent emotion of depression (C). It does, of course, seem quite logical and rational to conclude that failing the test caused the emotion. But this formula, in actuality, is not true, and it is not rational. Let's evaluate the equation to find out whether A really causes C.

To scientifically test whether or not failing an exam caused depression, we need to hypothetically try our experiment on a large cross-section of people. Let's imagine that we observed the consequent emotions of a thousand people who experienced the same failure. If all thousand people reacted exactly the same way to A, with feelings of unhappiness, sadness, or depression, then we could conclude that A appears to cause C.

In reminiscing about your days at school, perhaps you remember that different people reacted differently to failure. For the sake of example, let's assume that in our sample of a thousand people, some would experience unhappiness, sadness, or depression. At the same time, however, we know from experience that a few people would become angry about the same event, while others would react as **goal thinkers** and experience brief disappointment at first. They would then go ahead to develop a plan for improvement on the next exam (like studying harder). There may even be a few who would experience happiness at *C* because they will receive extra attention from the teacher.

Why is it that not everyone experiences the same emotions in reaction to the same stimulus (in this case, failing the exam)? The only explanation is that *A*, what happens to you in life, does not cause *C*, your emotions. Then what does cause your consequent emotions? If we asked each of the sample group why they felt the way they did, we would learn something quite interesting. And this is the point of rational thinking.

From the person who was depressed, we would hear something like:

> "I can't stand it. This is horrible. What a catastrophe, failing the test. I'm so depressed. I'm worthless." (Not provable, and thus not rational.)

From the person who was angry, we might hear something like:

> "I'm boiling. The questions were unfair. The teacher was just trying to do me in." (Not provable, and thus not rational.)

From the person who was just disappointed and went on to develop a new plan (*goal thinker*), we would hear:

> "I failed the test [a proven fact and thus rational]. That disappoints me. I'll have to work harder the next time. But I can do it. Instead of catastrophizing about the failure, I'll use my energies to get working on the next test." (Provable, and thus rational.)

The different emotional reactions to the same stimulus demonstrate that *A* does not cause *C*. *C*, then, must be caused by some other factor. This is where the *B* of rational thinking enters. *B* is a person's beliefs or what a person tells himself or herself about the activating events (*A*).

Very simply, your emotions are caused by your beliefs about what happens to you and not by the original experience that activated them. Remember Victor Frankl and Moorhead Kennedy, who experienced potentially overwhelming stress in their imprisoned situations? They coped because of their beliefs.

Activating event or experience

Belief or what you tell yourself about the event

Consequent emotions

Beliefs, not activating events, cause consequent emotions. And the wonderful news is that while you may not be in charge of what happens to you at *A,* you are in charge of the beliefs you develop toward the events in your life at *B*. **It is your beliefs that, in the end, cause your emotions.** Again, remember:

Your Rational Beliefs	*Create*	*Rational Emotions*	*Which In Turn Create*	*Rational Successful Actions (developing a plan, e.g., studying harder)*

At the crux between happiness and unhappiness or between success and failure are your beliefs. Rational thinking explains why some of your friends who appear to have everything in life are still unhappy and why other people who experience many stressful events in life choose happiness. It explains why a financially well-to-do person may commit suicide and an impoverished person may be the one who gives your spirits a lift. It's all in your beliefs or your view. By using the power of rational thinking, you can soar above any negative life experiences.

Application Of Rational Thinking Skills

Remind yourself that rational thinking is your link to success and happiness.

1. Just as you are what you eat, you are what you think. Think your way to success and happiness through scientifically provable, rational thinking.

2. Your thinking creates your emotions and your actions. Rational thinking also produces productive successful actions.

3. Build your rational muscle by practicing the A-B-C's of rational thinking:

   Activating event

   Beliefs about the event

   Consequent emotions

   Remember, your emotions are not caused by what happens to you at *A*; rather, your emotion at *C* is caused by your views or beliefs (*B*) about events. Change your beliefs and you change your life.

4. Achieve success and happiness by overcoming the worst disease of humankind—**perfectionism**. Have the courage to be imperfect, to take risks, and to grow. Live your life out of enjoyment instead of fear.

5. Achieve success and happiness by using your own stamp of approval. Waiting for everyone else's approval of your actions is like waiting to go skiing on the beaches of Acapulco. Trust yourself and you give yourself the greatest gift in the world.

6. Achieve success and happiness by living in the power of the present. Look to your right, look to your left, look up—but don't look back. You are alive at this moment. Capture it.

References

Ansbacher, H. and Rowena Ansbacher. *The Individual Psychology of Alfred Adler*. New York: Basic Books, 1956.

Ellis, A. and Robert Harper. *A New Guide to Rational Living*. North Hollywood, CA: Wilshire Books, 1975.

Frankl, Victor. *Man's Search for Meaning*. Boston, MA: Beacon Press, 1959.

15 Goal Commitment Skills To Define Your Destination

Have you ever noticed that the only ones who reach their dreams are those who have them? That's because you can't get anywhere unless you know where you are going.

Mike helps you get meaning out of your day, each day, every day. He encourages you to set a goal for the day and to make an unbending commitment to achieve it. "What would you like to make happen today?" exalts Mike. "Let's get started and seize the moment!" Or, "Dream big! What would be the ultimate goal you would like to achieve in your lifetime?" Mike encourages you to make the most out of each moment by identifying a goal. Mike would be a great leader because of his ability to encourage people to start dreaming.

Mike has goal commitment skills. By using the goal commitment skills in this chapter, you, too, will turn a random day into a day of purposeful achievement.

Have you ever noticed that the only ones who ever achieve their goals are those who have them? That's because without a destination, we play no role in our destiny. Our lives are either up to us or up to luck or chance. Positive people know where they are going. They have a goal. And they are committed to reaching it.

Letting The Power Of Your Goals Give You A Lift

For millions of years, Mount Everest, the highest peak on earth, towering majestically at 29,028 feet, stood as an unconquerable goal and the ultimate symbol of human challenge. Almost half a century ago, this snowcapped, 5.5-mile-high piece of natural architecture lost its claim to fame. Thanks to Sir Edmund Hillary and Lenzing Norgay, Mount Everest is no longer man's unconquerable challenge. On May 29, 1953, these two courageous men reached the summit once thought to be unattainable. In conquering Mount Everest, Hillary and Norgay not only accomplished what was once thought to be impossible but clearly illustrated the infiniteness and superiority of man's capabilities. Mount Everest now must look up to mankind.

Dramatic accomplishments such as the dangerous trek to the top of Mount Everest, the feasibility of shuttle service to various points in space, and the rapid advancement of technology attest to the fact that any human goal is achievable. Although achievements in these areas of endeavor may lie beyond your realm of interest, the process you use to accomplish your own goals is really the same as that used by the climbers, the engineers, and the scientists.

Creativity and enthusiasm, like an arrow, need a target; without a target, all effort is wasted. With a map, you can see your destination and can avoid many back roads and detours. **Lock your goals firmly in mind and go for them.** Then experience the enormous lifting power of your goals, because once you establish a goal firmly in your mind, it lifts you by finding the ways and means to achieve it.

The Goal Makes The Difference

Think about the following everyday examples of how the power of goal-setting works:

> A salesperson wants to advance in her company and establishes the goal of winning the big account.

A group of parents, concerned about the safety of their children, get together and establish a goal of having a traffic light installed near the neighborhood school.

An entrepreneur sees a need for a delicatessen in her community and sets the goal of opening one.

An executive in charge of quality control aims for a goal of 95% flawless product.

A teenage boy establishes a plan to win the student council election.

A high school student on the verge of failure establishes a goal of passing final exams.

Each of these people used the same process of goal achievement that the mountain climbers employed to bring about success. In each case, success began as a firm goal. Imagine what would have happened if these people had not taken a few moments to set goals. What if the salesperson had not taken some time to lock the goal of winning the big account firmly in mind? Most likely, she would never win the big account. No goal—no lifting power. What if the group of parents had not formally gotten together to set the goal of having a traffic light installed at the neighborhood intersection? A traffic light would probably never be installed and the intersection would remain just as dangerous. No goal—no lifting power. What if the entrepreneur had not established the goal of filling the need for a deli in her community? There would not be a deli until someone else set the goal. Without a goal locked firmly in mind, no success is possible.

Your goal, locked firmly in mind, makes the difference. Feed off the powerful lift that goal-setting gives you. The climbers who reached the top of Mount Everest and the salesperson determined to win the big account had a goal that gave them extra help. Their goal, like a magnet, attracted all of their actions.

How Do Goals Make The Difference And Give Lifting Power?

Consciously establishing your goals gives you at least three advantages over a person who wanders aimlessly. First, a goal subconsciously lifts you by forcing you, even in your sleep, to find ways to achieve it. Perhaps you have been determined to buy a new car, gain admission to college, or secure a new job. Did you find that you found a way to achieve your goal through your creativity? In addition to helping your creativity work for you, a firmly locked-in goal gives you a lift in another way. It gives you additional enthusiasm. Enthusiasm is the power and the energy to ignite your creative ideas into potential action. Many an underdog football team has beaten a bigger, stronger opponent because its goal of victory was more firmly locked in. When their goal was lifting them, they had more energy to make it happen. A third way that a firmly locked-in goal lifts you is by giving you direction when you are confused or lost. Goals show you where you are in relation to your destination of Success City.

Need A Lift?

Try an experiment to test the lifting power of firmly locked-in goals. Ask yourself this question: What city, resort, or vacation spot would I most like to visit within the next few years? Dream. Don't be shy. Would it be Hawaii, the pyramids of Egypt, the Orient, the Holy Land, the Rockies, the Grand Ole Opry in Nashville, Rio? Allow your mind to flow freely.

Four Ways To Be A Responsible Goal-Oriented Thinker

1. Act, don't catastrophize. When your car runs out of gas, don't ask why or accuse life. Instead, find a way to get more gas and move on to your destination. When your boss tells you that you will lose your sales position in six months unless you increase your sales, make a plan. Take a sales course, make every appointment you schedule, and work triple hard. Become the successful salesperson your boss has never seen. Your new thoughts and views will make the difference in your success. Contrast that successful style with the catastrophizing, blaming style.

2. Take charge of all the power you have within you by the way you look at things. Regardless of how challenging circumstances may be, don't spend your time accusing. Spend your time dealing with the problem, taking responsibility, setting new winning goals, and moving toward those goals.

3. Get on course. An airplane doesn't travel in a straight line from one city to another. The pilot makes a series of calculations and adjustments along the way. When the plane gets off course, the pilot simply gets it back on course. It's the same way with you and your goals. Get to your destination by following the same pattern for success. When you get off course (failure, rejection, mistakes), don't become an *ego thinker*, simply get back on course. Your goal is awaiting your arrival.

4. Imbed these few words of wisdom in your heart and you will reach home plate every time. The four maxims are: (1) How I got to where I am today is irrelevant. (2) The past is the past. (3) Where I go tomorrow is up to me. (4) **It's up to me to develop a goal and take advantage of the lifting power of that goal.**

Avoiding The Failure Trap On The Way To Your Goals: Lacking Goals To Give Yourself A Lift

Cheshire Cat: "What's the matter, little girl? May I help you?"

Alice: "I'm lost. I don't know which road to take."

Cheshire Cat: "Well, where is it that you would like to go?"

Alice: "I don't know."

Cheshire Cat: "Well, if you don't know where you'd like to go, it doesn't much matter which road you take."

(Paraphrased from *Alice in Wonderland*)

Alice did not have a goal to lift her. She was wandering aimlessly; she was lost. Even if she had a map, it wouldn't have made any difference because she had no destination. If she were destined to go any place, she was destined for no place. Observe how successes differ from failures in the way people talk about their goals:

Failures	Successes
"I *should* get the car washed to-day." (Tentative goal not firmly locked in mind, and consequently has no lifting power)	"I'm definitely getting my car washed in the Washarama at ten o'clock." (Goal firmly locked in and consequently has lifting power)
"Maybe someday I'll stop smoking. Smoking isn't the best thing for a person." (Very tentative)	"I'm quitting smoking right now by not having a cigarette all day. (Firm goal)

Who will most likely succeed—the person who takes advantage of his or her goals or the person who "shoulds," "coulds," or "maybes" his or her way around the commitment to a firm goal?

When you firmly lock a goal in your mind, all of your feelings, thoughts, and actions begin to work for you to help you achieve your goal. Psychiatrists point out that all behavior has a purpose or a goal. Either you take charge of your goal or it takes charge of you. When you lock a goal firmly in mind, every one of your feelings, thoughts, and actions comes under your subconscious control. When you fail to develop a firm goal, your unrealized goals take over.

In *You Can Do It: How to Encourage Yourself,* Losoncy (1980, pp. 38–40) introduces the concept of the unrealized goal:

Although you are the executive of all of your feelings, thoughts, and actions, most of the time you fail to make your goals clear. And when you fail to develop clear goals, other unrealized goals may take over. Remember that your feelings, thoughts, and actions are constantly being pulled by either your firm goals or your unrealized goals.

Unrealized goals are a talented and formidable opponent to you. Short-term satisfaction is one example of an unrealized goal that can snatch your employees (your feelings, thoughts, and actions) right from under you! Consider Ethel, whose firm goal is to lose weight. Observe the struggle between her unrealized goal and her firm goal as she is confronted with a high-calorie ice cream cake just after she has finished a big meal!

Unrealized Goal:	*Firm Goal:*
I want this ice cream cake now.	I want to lose weight.
Feelings:	*Feelings:*
It makes me so angry. Why do I have to be so heavy? It just isn't fair. It's so depressing when I look in a mirror. Well, I'm so bad off, what more will a little ice cream cake hurt?	I feel so good that I can walk away from this ice cream cake. And if I think I feel good now, just think how good I'll feel if I lose those 10 pounds because of sacrifices like this.
Thinking:	*Thinking:*
It shouldn't be this hard to diet. Just this one time won't hurt.	It's difficult to turn this down, but I can stand it.
It's unfair. My sister can eat all she wants, and I just look at food, and I gain weight. Heck, I'm not going to deprive myself of this food.	My sister is fortunate, because she can eat all she wants. That has nothing to do with me, however.
I deserve this ice cream cake. Look how hard I worked all week.	I might deserve the cake. It would taste good for about five minutes. But then I have to live with its effects. It isn't worth it and it directly interferes with my goals.
I'll start my diet tomorrow instead.	I have control now, and it won't be any easier tomorrow.
Actions:	*Actions:*
Ethel eats the ice cream cake, and the unrealized goal wins out.	Ethel walks away from the ice cream cake. The firm goal wins out.

Identify some unrealized goals in your past that have generally won the battle. Remember, you as a human being are so powerful that you decide the winner. Successful people are those who direct their feelings, thoughts, and actions toward their firm goals. They state their goal, know their resources, and mobilize their feelings, thoughts, and actions into the desired directions, and they defeat their unrealized goals.

...Courageous people take advantage of the constant pulling power of their positive goals.

Develop Firm Goals And Be The Chief Executive Of Your Life

If you feel like your thoughts, feelings, and actions are out of your control, you have become your own worst enemy and a slave to your unrealized goals. You have chosen to be a pawn rather than the chief executive of your life. Rise up and overthrow your feelings of powerlessness. Put yourself where you belong—in charge of your life. You can do it right now by doing one simple thing. Firmly lock in a destination for yourself and write it down. Then watch the unmatched power of your goals lift you to them, like the top of Mount Everest called the mountain climbers!

Application Of Goal Commitment Skills

1. Every time you establish a goal and lock it in as firmly as Sir Edmund Hillary and Lenzig Norgay locked in their goal of climbing Mount Everest, you give yourself lifting power. The more firmly the goal is locked in, the greater the lift.

2. Let the power of your goals give you a lift to success by being a **goal thinker** rather than an **ego thinker**. Make your goals more important than your ego. Give credit to anyone who

gives you an idea, even when it differs from your own idea. Welcome criticism. Make defeat sweet by the powers of **goal thinking**. Finally, build your self-image by "elevating your competition."

3. Let the power of your goals give you a lift to success by being a **responsible, goal-oriented thinker** rather than an accusation thinker. Spend your valuable life energies dealing with the obstacles instead of tracking down the source of blame. When you get a flat tire, don't accuse life or the highway system. Fix the flat and move on. When you find yourself straying from a goal through failure, rejection, or mistakes, become a **destination, goal-oriented thinker**. Correct the mistake and get back on course. Be a responsible person by sizing up any situation, no matter how difficult, and daring to say, "It's up to me to develop a firm goal and take advantage of its lifting power."

4. Let the power of your goals give you a lift to success by realizing that what is is. This powerful insight will help you overcome life entangled in a "wisher's web" or a traffic jam on the Fairness Freeway. Get off of the Sea of Fantasy and move to the Coast of Reality by eliminating all "shoulds," "oughts," and "musts" from your vocabulary. Like all successful people do, say, **"What's my plan?"** instead of saying should or shouldn't.

5. Finally, let the power of your goals lift you to success by firmly locking in your goals. Be the chief executive of your life by taking charge of your goals and avoiding the powerless feeling of being ruled by your unrealized goal. You can do it!

Reference

Losoncy, Lewis. *You Can Do It!* New York: Simon & Schuster, 1980.

16

Optimism Skills To Find The Best Vantage Point

Emily believes that anything is possible. "No problem," is Emily's answer to any request. Emily believes that the answer to every single problem lies in the alive, creative mind of a determined person. "Of course we can increase our sales by 25%," Emily shouts. "After all, if we can put a man on the moon, we can find ways to do more. No problem."

Emily has a tremendous advantage over most of the rest of the world. Whereas others become frustrated, discouraged, and ready to give up when facing an obstacle for which they believe there is no solution, Emily is lifted by the insight that every problem has a solution. Don't you wish Emily was working to find a cure for cancer or solve world hunger?

Emily has optimism skills. The world needs more people with the optimism skills that Emily has. In this chapter, you will develop your skills in believing that every problem has a solution. No problem!

The positive person has many advantages in life, none more evident than when the creative optimist experiences what to many would be a crisis, or even a setback. The positive person views a setback in a way that will keep him or her going...and going...and going! The positive person knows that belief is everything. Believing is seemingly magical because believing creates visions and expectations of what can—and will—be. Believing that things can be improved and setbacks can be overcome is motivating. Beliefs are the seeds to grow our new future.

The power of belief has been known throughout history. Two thousand years ago, the Stoic philosopher Epictetus proclaimed, "We are not disturbed by things, but only by our belief about things." As discussed in Chapter 14 on rational thinking skills, our beliefs are even more important than external events.

Henry Ford proclaimed, "Believe you can or believe you can't; either way you'll be correct."

The philosopher Baruch Spinoza wrote, "For as long as you believe a certain goal impossible, for that exact period of time it will be impossible." And we add, the moment you believe the dream to be possible, at that very moment you take your first, and most important, step toward the dream. Achieving starts with believing—believing you can rise above where you are now.

Dr. Jonas Salk warned us to never make the mistake of limiting the vision of our future by the narrow experience of our past. The past is over if we believe it to be over. Writer John Dryden concluded that when there is no hope or belief, there can be no endeavor. When there is no endeavor, there can be no achievement. Great things start with hope and belief. The optimist has the advantage because the optimist believes.

Belief is more important than our experiences. Alfred Adler explained that neither heredity nor environment is the ultimate determinant of who we are. They are only the building blocks out of which we construct the person we choose to become. Our beliefs are the architects of those building blocks, arranging them to either build our future or tear it down.

How Do Optimistic Beliefs Work?

Optimistic beliefs give a positive person three advantages. First, believing gives us the courage to face our perceived limitations and fears. When we face our greatest fears, motivated by the power of belief, we find we can overcome them. Then we know we can do the same in the future, so we stop worrying because we know that we can handle whatever will come our way.

A second reason why optimistic beliefs work is because believing helps us realize that we can be more of a person tomorrow than we are today. We tend to become the person who we believe we are. Believing, then, enhances our self-image.

On the topic of self-image, Maxwell Maltz (1960) wrote:

> The self-image is the key to the personality and human behavior. Change the self-image and the personality and you change your behavior. But even more than this, the self-image sets the boundaries of individual achievement. It defines what you can and cannot be. Expand the self-image and you expand the area of the possible. The development of an adequately realistic self-image will seem to imbue the individual with new talents, new capabilities and literally turn failure into success.

Third, believing opens up our creative determination to unleash the stored potential in our unlimited minds.

When you believe in yourself, you (1) have more courage to face your fears, (2) expand your self-image because you know that who you can be has little to do with who you were, and (3) draw from the unlimited creativity in your subconscious mind.

Can you think of any argument not to believe?

Optimism Skills: Going To The Best Vantage Point

Driving through the beautiful mountains of reality, there are always places that provide better, clearer views. The positive person finds those viewpoints or vantage points that maximize what he or she can experience. A better viewpoint can be found in both up and down lifescapes. A positive person with the skills of optimism is a person with the will and the skill to create a flow and maximize the moment.

Some skills of optimism include: (1) positive environmental engineering and (2) optimistic explanatory skills.

1. Positive Environmental Engineering

Congratulations! We have great news for you! You have just been hired for one of the most prestigious professional positions in the world. We are pleased to announce that today you begin your new post as Director of Environmental Engineering for the most important account in the world—your own.

Just as the air you breathe in from your physical environment affects your physical health, your psychological environment affects your psychological health. When pollution levels are high, the negative contaminants you breathe in circulate throughout your body. When the negative thought pollution in your environment is high, it is difficult for you to be a creative, enthusiastic, goal-directed person.

Take charge today. Engineer a mass cleanup of your attitude environment by eliminating polluted thinking. Create a fresh, idea-inspiring, spring morning feeling in your surroundings. Then watch your creative ideas, powered by your enthusiasm, flow into successful actions.

Your Environment Is Also A Product Of You

Your environment is a powerful influence on you. In fact, the most popular school of psychological thought in the 1960s was Behavioral Psychology, usually credited to the brilliant B.F. Skinner. Behaviorists, as the advocates of Skinner's view were called, argued that people are a product of their environment. Human behavior could be understood simply by understanding a person's environment. To change behavior, the behavioral engineer would simply alter the environment.

An environment with an abundance of encouragement tends to invite positive behavior, whereas a negative environment tends to invite discouragement. While environment is important, a person is not totally and helplessly a product of his or her environment. In fact, the opposite is even truer; that is, your environment is a *product of you*. This powerful view asserts that you are an active creator of your environment rather than just a passive marionette dangling from the strings of the mentality of the people around you.

If you doubt that you play a role in creating your environment, try a simple test. The next time you go to a restaurant, give a warm smile to you waiter or waitress. Observe the reaction of your server to this positive approach. Now approach another server with a gruff "Where were you? I've been waiting for a long time!" Contrast the two responses you receive and see if the environmental reactions differ when you change your style.

Yes, you are Director of Environmental Engineering for the construction of a positive setting for success for yourself. And the great news is that you have many, many people and unlimited natural resources to assist you in developing a winning environment. Your new environment can start and end on a positive note.

Designing An Environment To Work For You:
Eight Positive Strategies

Put positive people in your environment

Overlook small negatives in your environment

Switch the big negatives into positives

Influence positively the environments of other people

Treasure what you already have as part of your life

Intellectually stimulate yourself by "ideating up" your environment

Vacation you mind and your senses in new environments

Expose yourself to positive media

Put Positive People In Your Environment

Raise your ecological standards. No longer allow yourself to be a dumping site for rotten reasoning, noxious negativism, or poisonous perceptions. Stop feeding your thoughts on the failure fodder so plentiful in environmental dumping sites. Lower the pollution index in your environment.

The first step in your environmental engineering cleanup is to surround yourself with the most positive people you know. When you do, you will become more creative, more enthusiastic, and more goal-centered, and you will even develop a more positive self-image. Negative people in your environment, who constantly point out everything that's wrong with life, make it easy for you to get down on life. And when you get down on life, you feel negative about yourself.

Most negative people can be easily recognized and quickly diagnosed. Engineer out of your environment people who use opening lines like:

> "I shouldn't tell you what people are saying about you and your ideas, but..."

> "Let me play devil's advocate for a minute..."

> "You never were very good at..."

> "I wouldn't waste my time with that idea of yours..."

> "You! You could never..."

Also stay away from people who always have tragic, doomsday news or people who are worried about the sun running out of energy in the next seven billion years.

When people focus on the negatives in life or on your negative behaviors, they are trying to lead you down Loser's Lane to show you where they live.

Issue A Warning To The World Of Negative Thinkers: Cease And Desist!

Negative people who try to bully themselves into your attitude ecology system need to be restrained. Tell them to cease and desist or you will have them arrested for first-degree mind-slaughter. Taking advice from negative failures is like hiring someone who has declared bankruptcy as your financial advisor. As Director of Environmental Engineering for yourself, you have the right and the obligation to remove toxic thinking. Your ulcers, migraines, hypertension, and depression may be related to the tension and stress that come from being influenced by negative thinkers. Clean up your thoughts and give a sensitive but stern warning to negative-thinking people:

> "I find that the last few times we were together, I walked away upset."

> "I felt discouraged the other day when we talked, and I think that it would be best if we didn't talk when you are feeling negative. However, I'd love to get together again when you are feeling more positive."

A few comments, stated not aggressively but firmly and fairly, will help not only you but, in fact, the negative person as well. Odds are that the next time you see your friend, he or she will have a big, cheery, positive smile.

Successful environmental engineering involves, first, putting negative people on probation and, second, hiring positive consultants to help you design your environment for success.

Hire A Board Of Positive Consultants To Help Design Your Environment

Don't take on a challenge as important as designing your environment by yourself. As Director of Environmental Engineering, you have the power not only to de-hire but to hire people to assist you. Hire you own board of free advisors to be part of your supersuccessfully stimulating environment.

The simplest task in the world is selecting the people who will be on your board of positive consultants. Identify at least five people based on the following qualifications: (1) you feel positive about yourself and life when you are with them, (2) you feel courageously willing to try new experiences and take new risks when you are with them, and (3) you feel free to speak and share even your craziest new ideas in their presence. Take this important exercise to heart. Jot down the names of the people you have honored as your selections. In your environment, **a positive friend is like a rare gem**.

When you have identified the people you would like on your board of advisors, make a point of telling each person that you have read a book on the importance of having positive consultants. Tell each person the three requirements for being a positive advisor and that you have selected him or her for the position. Then ask each of your choices to consider accepting a position on your advisory board and express your confidence in the fact that acceptance involves nothing more than continuing to be himself or herself. Your comments will elate all of them to no end. How would you feel if someone complimented you by saying that out of everyone he or she knew, you were one of the most positive influences on his or her life? After you share your news, you will find that these people are rarely "down" in your presence.

Become determined to spend more time with each of your board members in the future. Make plans to see them and talk with them, even if only on the telephone. When you consider the fact that people pay over $100 an hour to talk with a psychiatrist or listen to a motivational lecturer, friends who help you feel positive are worth quite a lot. Don't neglect positive advisors, your richest source of input.

And the great news is that even if you can't be near your board of advisors because of distance or timing, it doesn't matter. When facing a difficult decision or a challenging situation, recall your advisors' thinking by visualizing their reactions to the event. In your imagination, confront each positive person with the situation and picture each one's response and advice. You will find the results of their advice to be quite interesting, if not incredible. Most of your advisors will probably agree on the best course of action for you! As Director of Environmental Engineering for yourself, hire the most positive people you know and watch your positive self-image grow.

Now, add an honorary board of advisors made up of the most inspirational thinkers in the world.

Appoint An Honorary Board Of Advisors For Yourself

Don't limit your advisory board to people you know. Add to your list people whom you respect, even if you don't know them personally. Allow us to share with you some of the people on Lew Losoncy's honorary board of environmental advisors. Lew's board has ten members, all of them successful people, and he provides balance by including both liberal and conservative advisors:

Lew Losoncy
Director of Environmental Engineering
Honorary Board of Advisors

Conservative Members	*Liberal Members*
Courageous Achievers	*Creative Envisioners*
Dr. Jonas Salk (discovered cure for polio)	The ant who moved the rubber tree plant in the song "High Hopes"
Arnie and Sydell Miller (founders of Matrix Essentials)	The Little Engine That Could ("I think I can, I think I can.")
Irvin Westheimer (founder of Big Brothers)	Annie, from the play *Annie* ("The Sun'll Come Out Tomorrow")
Orville and Wilbur Wright	

When Lew needs advice, he consults with each of the members of his board and asks, "What would you do if you were faced with this challenge?" He has received some powerful and successful advice from these board members. Just imagine the combined advice you could receive from your honorary board and your regular board of advisors. Imagine how much more likely you will be to succeed than people who surround themselves with negative people.

Surround Yourself With People Who Have Behaviors, Traits, Or Thoughts That You Want To Develop

The best way to learn Spanish is to go to a country where the people speak Spanish and associate with them! Associate with people who act like you want to.

Lew Losoncy noticed something very interesting about a charismatic executive of a Chicago car rental company. Not only did he have an unusual beard with no mustache, but he also had unusual hand and facial mannerisms. While these aspects of his appearance were not all that interesting in themselves, what was very interesting was that some of the people working with him also had the same unusual beard and mannerisms. The employees identified with their boss. You tend to become similar to the people with whom you surround yourself.

Did you ever find yourself imitating the mannerisms, speech, or vocabulary of others? Recently, Lew Losoncy was in Wetaskiwin, Alberta. Interestingly, after spending only four weeks there, he found himself saying "eh" at the end of his sentences, a colloquialism characteristic of many Canadians. Surround yourself with people who have behavior traits and thoughts you like or admire. With little if any personal effort, you will start to develop their characteristics.

If you want to quit smoking, make sure that you spend a great deal of time in the environment of nonsmokers. If you want to stop procrastinating, surround yourself with prompt, responsible people. If you want to get rid of your depression, surround yourself with positive people.

Start your environmental engineering plan by: (1) issuing a "cease and desist" warning to the negative thinkers around you, (2) identifying the most positive people you know and placing them on your board of environmental advisors, (3) creating an honorary board of advisors from the world's most inspirational people, and (4) surrounding yourself with people who have behaviors, traits, and thoughts that you want to develop.

After putting positive people in your environment, use the second strategy in your engineering plan—overlook the small negatives.

Expose Yourself To Positive Media

Just as the air you breathe affects your health, negative media, whether television, radio, or newspapers, affects your attitude. Wipe out the media pollution from your life. One of the easiest ways to get the wrong picture of life is to blindly accept all that you see in the media as truth. Sometimes a report or story can be very one-sided.

A few years ago, Lew Losoncy was in a midwestern city to speak at a high school graduation. On the way to the school, his inquisitive cab driver asked him what brought him to the Midwest. Lew explained that he was there to speak to the high school graduates about how to positively think their way to success. The cab driver slowed his car and, peering through the rear view mirror, sneered, "Teenagers and positive attitudes. Huh! I'll tell you about teenagers. Did you see the headline of today's paper?" He showed Lew the paper; the headline read something like "Two Boys Caught Starting Warehouse Fire." The cab driver added, "That's the kind of kids we have today."

Taken aback by the cab driver's conclusion, Lew asked, "How many kids do you have in your city?" "Oh, about forty thousand," the cab driver said. Lew responded, "Forty thousand! Why, sir, if I were creating the headline for today's newspaper, the same story would have read, 'Rejoice! 39,998 Of Our Children Not Caught Starting A Fire Last Night.' That's 99.99%. The headline reflected less than one ten-thousandth of the truth." The cab driver had treated the headline as though that's the way all kids are. Incredible!

Lew shared his experience in the cab with western Pennsylvania school superintendents and board members. One of the school superintendents, Dr. Leo Bourandas, from Butler, Pennsylvania, picked up on the idea, and a few weeks later sent Lew a copy of the *Butler Eagle* newspaper. The headline read, "School Superintendent Cites Good Kids." As Lew read the article, he was elated to see that in every category of discipline, more than 99% of the students had not violated the rules. Wouldn't you make the *Butler Eagle* your newspaper?

2. Optimistic Explanatory Skills

Along with positive environmental engineering skills, the positive person uses optimistic explanatory skills. In his book *Learned Optimism,* the upbeat and practical psychologist Martin Seligman (1991) outlined a breakthrough concept in optimism. Seligman studied how optimists and pessimists explain setbacks to themselves in dramatically different ways. He called how we explain a setback our "explanatory style." Seligman's ideas are powerful and can change your life in one reading.

There are three major differences in how optimists and pessimists explain a setback to themselves. Pessimists tend to take the viewpoint that setbacks are personal, permanent, and pervasive. That is, when something happens to a pessimist, such as a rejection or not getting a job, the pessimist concludes: (1) "I'm no good" (personal), (2) "I'll never be any good" (permanent), and (3) "I'll never be any good at anything" (pervasive). Imagine how you would feel if every time you experienced a setback, you took these viewpoints toward your setback. Would you ever even try anything again? Probably not.

The positive person, or optimist, tends to use a different explanatory style to respond to the same setback. The optimist, after refection, takes these vantage points: (1) "The situation wasn't right" (situation-related instead of personal), (2) "I'll get the next job" (temporary rather than permanent), and (3) "It won't affect any other area of my life" (not pervasive, just situation-related).

Imagine the lifting advantage that optimistic explanatory skills can provide. By viewing a setback optimistically, we are urged to go forward, rather than catastrophize and give up. As a positive person, you are encouraged to read *Learned Optimism* by Seligman.

Your beliefs shape your destiny. The optimist, who holds go forward beliefs, goes forward. There is no down-side risk to being an optimist, as long as you have life. You can be positive about that.

Application Of Optimism Skills To Keep That Positive Flow

1. When in doubt, choose to believe. Raise your standards. Think bigger and better.

2. Become Director of Positive Environmental Engineering for yourself:

   Put positive people in your life

   Overlook small negatives in your environment

   Switch the big negatives into positives

   Influence positively the environments of others

   Treasure what you already have

   Intellectually stimulate yourself by "ideating up" your environment

   Vacation your mind and your senses in new environments

   Expose yourself to positive media

3. Practice taking an optimistic vantage point toward setbacks; they are situation-related and temporary, not personal, permanent, or pervasive.

References

Losoncy, Lewis. *You Can Do It!* New York: Simon & Schuster, 1980.

Losoncy, Lewis. *Think Your Way to Success*. North Hollywood, CA: Wilshire Books, 1982.

Maltz, Maxwell. *Psychocybernetics*. North Hollywood, CA: Wilshire Books, 1960.

Seligman, Martin. *Learned Optimism*. New York: Knopf, 1991.

17

Positive Leadership Skills

Y ou can get anything you want in life if you simply help everyone else to get what they want. A person with positive leadership skills knows that quite well. Sydell is a positive leader. She combines the skills of listening, responding, agreement, believing, enthusiasm, asset focusing, perceptual alternatives, humor, rational thinking, goal commitment, and optimism by using each one at just the right time. She tells her team, "Many people think that the odds are stacked against us. But we know what we have to do. We know our strengths. And we know something else. We are not going to stop until we reach our dream together. By next year we will be number one. The only thing that can stop us is us. Let history record that we began at this moment on a journey that turned an average bunch of individuals into a team that became the best there was at what it did. Let us begin now!"

Sydell has positive leadership skills. In this chapter, you will put all of your skills together and become a positive leader!

Observe groups of people. Find the leaders. They are the ones who get things done. Leaders not only achieve their own goals but, even more importantly, know how to help other people achieve their goals. Leaders are those rare people who walk, talk, feel, think, and act with positive purpose. Being a leaders is not a talent, as some suggest. It is not something that a person is born with. Leadership books like *The Motivating Team Leader* and *Teamwork Makes the Dream Work* prove that anyone can be a leader. When a person develops the skills in this chapter and couples them with the skills from the previous chapters, leadership develops.

Your leadership skills can be employed in every social setting. Watch how leaders act wherever you go. As you watch leaders, you will learn that the true leader is not necessarily the one who talks the most; he or she is the one who keeps the group on course and keeps everyone energized. You can observe leadership in operation every time two or more people get together to tackle a task.

A family decides to make their own pasta for the first time, and the teenage son asks, "What would be the best way to do this?" This key question encourages the family members to brainstorm about each member's talents. Mom is good at mixing things the right way so she could mix the dough. Susan can measure the ingredients. Dad can cut the dough, and so on. Progress occurred because the leader asked the right questions to make things happen. Each family member had a purpose, a goal, a direction, rather than wandering aimlessly around the kitchen. In this instance, the teenage son's question made him a leader. Soon the family will enjoy the pasta together, and each will feel a sense of accomplishment from his or her role in the task. The leader makes the difference by taking things off dead center.

A vice-president of an engineering firm calls his staff of engineers together to describe a difficult task facing them. He encourages the group to think of the specific talents of each of the professionals in order to build a team to tackle the challenge. The selected members are motivated because their peers demonstrated confidence in them. The complex project is successfully completed because of the leadership skill of the vice-president. The leadership style made the difference and made things move.

Observe leaders in every social situation. They help to *create* solutions rather than dictate them. Leaders create a successful atmosphere by raising key questions, encouraging people to recognize the talents and resources among the group members, and motivating the group to stay on course to achieve their goals. Watch leaders. You will find that true leaders who last as leaders use the powerful approach of encouragement.

How To Think Like A Leader

Start your own leadership development program now by reinforcing some of the skills you have learned and adding some new ones. Develop the skills that the most successful leaders in the world have and enlist the support of others by thinking like a leader. Become a leader by:

Listening with full attention

Empathizing with people

Asset focusing

Developing alternative perceptions

Encouraging team spirit

Recognizing the power of conveying confidence in people

The First Skill Of A Leader: Listening With Full Attention

First and foremost, leaders are effective listeners. They give full attention to the speaker's concerns, feelings, and theme. How refreshing it is to be with someone who really listens to you and gives you the ultimate human gifts—time and attention. The listener not only gains respect and popularity in your eyes but learns more as well. No wonder listeners become sought as leaders.

There is a science to effective listening. Every conversation you engage in is a golden opportunity for you to build your listening skills. Through practice, the skill of effective listening will become natural to you. Listen your way to leadership.

Listen Your Way To The Top

Improve your relationships with everyone and find yourself being a leader by becoming a more effective listener. Avoid playing such games as "Can you top this?" and "Oh, that's nothing! Wait until I tell you what happened to me!" Literally change your personal relationships in one day by using the listening skills that leaders have.

1. Create a setting that shows the speaker that you are involved and fully attentive. Be there! Effective listening is like dancing with the speaker's words. Smile with the humorous words, have heightened energies with the enthusiastic words, show concern with the troublesome words, and display an openness for controversial words. Practice being there!

2. Be a fully attentive listener by making eye contact. A helpful way of showing you are present in a relationship is through your eyes. Effective listeners have the ability to use an ideal amount of eye contact. What is an ideal amount? Obviously, too little or no eye contact might convey disinterest or lack of involvement. On the other hand, constant staring may be threatening and produce defensiveness in the speaker. The ideal amount of eye contact is the amount you feel comfortable with while avoiding frequent breaks.

In your next few interactions with people, become sensitive to the listening power in your eyes. Improve your eye contact by looking in a mirror and see what others see. Feel the encouragement power in your eyes!

3. Be a fully attentive listener by showing your presence through your body language. Our body posture and gestures give clues to our presence or absence in a relationship. Tense or closed posture with distracting gestures tends to disrupt the easy flow of communication.

What pet annoyances (habits or mannerisms) have you experienced while speaking that have stopped your train of thought? Was the listener yawning or looking beyond you, with arms rigidly folded, stern eyebrows, and frequent movements like tapping his or her feet. Practice avoiding these distancing gestures. Listen your way to the top by showing a relaxed, nonthreatening, open (arms and heart) posture. Every single time you are with a person is an opportunity to develop your "I am here" body language.

4. Be a fully attentive listener by sensitively unraveling the speaker's theme. Proceed in every conversation with the thought that the speaker has a theme. The theme may not always be apparent, and sometimes you will need to "reach into" the speaker's words. Listen unselfishly and noninterferingly to the words and, even more important, the feelings behind the words. Avoid the natural tendency to think, "How does what this person is saying affect me?"

Listening to the theme involves staying on the topic that the other person starts rather than introducing a new one. It also involves trying to look at the world through other people's eyes and hearing the world through other people's ears. After listening with their full attention, leaders use the second skill of communication—they respond to the speaker's comments with empathy.

The Second Skill Of A Leader: Empathizing With People

Have you ever found yourself caught in a conversation and not knowing what to say next? Knowing how to respond is very simple, and you can develop your skills in responding in just a few seconds. Avoid being caught in the "mouthtrap," and make the following ideas part of your regular response style.

1. Respond empathically, instead of judgmentally, to the speaker's words and feelings. Most people are all too eager to tell you what you should have done. But who will listen to you with understanding? Not many people. That's why true leaders have the skill of empathic listening and responding. What does empathic responding involve?

First, empathic responding is listening without judging or evaluating the speaker's words. Every time you judge ("You're right" or "You're wrong"), you stop the message and create barriers that keep the speaker's full meaning from being communicated. This only frustrates the speaker. Every day, remind yourself to listen and not to immediately judge the words and ideas of others. The most challenging times for you to be nonjudgmental are when you have strong emotions or strong opinions about what the speaker is saying.

You gain an unequaled and powerful ability to lead and motivate the minute that you force yourself to hear, feel, and sense the speaker's words from his or her perspective.

2. Respond empathically by turning the speaker's words into feelings.

On Lew Losoncy's first visit to Edmonton, Alberta, he received a wake-up call from a cheery Canadian hotel employee. She enlightened him with a bright, "Good morning, sir! It's seven a.m. and the temperature is zero! Have a great day." Zero degrees outside! Lew panicked. An hour later in the same hotel, still not having faced the outside, he addressed a convention of the Alberta Teacher's Association and shared with the group his startled reaction to the wake-up call.

Following his talk, one of the teachers stopped him and said, "Don't let the zero temperature scare you. That's in centigrade." And like a computer she reassuringly added, "Zero degrees centigrade is equal to thirty-two degrees Fahrenheit." Lew immediately took two of his sweaters off! He had failed to convert the temperature from centigrade to Fahrenheit and had made an inaccurate assumption. The young teacher had the ability to immediately translate one scale into the other. You might say that she had empathy for Lew's view and helped him because of it.

Leaders with empathy have the same translation talent. But instead of changing centigrade into Fahrenheit, empathic people have the ability to spontaneously turn a person's words into feelings. This ability to translate is rare indeed. Always remember that the secret of listening empathically is turning words into feelings.

While delivering a motivational lecture in Des Moines, Iowa, Lew Losoncy asked a group of about 2000 people what they would say if their first-grade son came home from school and said, "That mean teacher yelled at me in front of all the kids!" In unison, he heard 2000 people shout a typical parent response: "What did you do?" He then asked the group what the child would say in response to "What did you do?" and the 2000 midwesterners declared, "Nothing." The parents' judgmental "What did you do?" yielded "nothing," literally. Communication had broken down.

Now watch the power of empathic responding, of turning the child's words into feelings. Listen very carefully to the words that capture a six-year-old's ears, eyes, and heart:

> "That mean teacher yelled at me in front of all the other kids."

Don't look at the words. Instead, see and hear the feelings behind the words. Look at the child's statement again and try to find at least three possible feelings. You might see embarrassment, hurt, anger, fear, or even guilt. Be truly creative in listening for feelings and find some more possible feelings. Now watch how the conversation can flow more easily by turning the words into feelings instead of judging them.

> *Child:* "That mean teacher yelled at me in front of all the other kids."
>
> *Empathic parent:* "It sure hurts to be yelled at in front of your friends, doesn't it?"
>
> *Child* (wiping his or her eyes): "Yeah."
>
> *Empathic parent:* "Would you like to tell me more about it?"
>
> *Child:* "Okay."

Succeed by turning a person's words into feelings. Make a plan to truly listen. First, understand instead of immediately judging people. Second, turn people's words into feelings. Now glance through the following Leadership Listening Style Reminder List. Keep it with you wherever you go and you will have a good friend.

Leadership Listening Style Reminder List

Take one minute each morning to review this list in preparation for the day.

- Stay on the speaker's topic.

- Give people attention and time.

- Don't be frightened by silences.

- Employ the word "you" or, even better, use the person's name occasionally.

- Keep thinking, "What does what this person is saying mean to him or her?" instead of "How does this affect me?"

- Be a mirror—show people that what they say is what they get.

- Don't play "Can you top this?" or "That reminds me of..." games.

- Don't react out of your own needs.

- Avoid interruptions.

- When listening, don't conclude where people are going before they get there.

- Think how your response will be viewed by the other person.

Ask yourself the following additional questions about what you say:

1. How does what I said fit in with what the other person said?

2. How does it relate to the other person's world?

3. Does it have any interest to the other person?

4. At what level have I responded to the other person's level?

5. How did what I said show the other person that he or she contributed to what I said?

6.   How did what I said contribute to continuing rather than ending the conversation?

7.   What does what I said mean about you and me?

8.   How honest is what I said?

9.   In what possible ways might what I said be interpreted?

10. Did I encourage the other person by what I said?

11. How did I demonstrate that I listened to the other person?

12. Have I physically demonstrated that I listened to the other person?

13. How did I sound? Was I enthusiastic?

14. Was the other person more encouraged or more discouraged by what I said?

Now continue your personal leadership development program by incorporating into your style the third skill of successful leaders: asset focusing.

The Third Skill Of A Leader: Asset Focusing

In addition to listening with full attention and empathizing with people, another essential skill in leadership is being able to spotlight and magnify an individual's strengths, assets, and resources. We all know people who are nit-pickers and flaw-finders, who focus on spotting a mistake, a weakness, or something which isn't as it "should" be. They are often quick to offer criticism. Be an individual who is finely tuned to hearing and seeing assets.

1. Develop your skills in asset focusing by conditioning yourself to immediately zero in on the assets in people you meet. Lew Losoncy often watches the person he considers to be the greatest encourager in the world—his father. After retiring from his regular work, his dad was so popular that he was elected constable in his community. A constable, as you may know, serves warrants, makes arrests, takes prisoners to court, etc. It may sound like a difficult and unrewarding job, but that's not the case for Lew's father. He loves his work and rarely has a problem eliciting the cooperation of the offenders. What is his secret of success?

Simple. The common sense psychologist (who has never taken a psychology course) humbly explains, "My job is to get people to cooperate. So when I visit people's homes with a warrant, I start by imagining I am in their shoes. When I do that, I know that if I were them, I would be anxious, try to hide, or even resist. So I'm easy, not forceful with them. I may say something like, 'I guess you feel I've come here to hassle you. I can understand your feelings.' Then, I compliment them on some asset. I look for something positive and ask something like, 'I see you have some trophies over your fireplace. Did you win them?' After discussing the trophies or some other positive quality the person has, I find the person is more open to talk. Then I tell them the details of why I am there and how it would work in their favor to cooperate rather than live in a state of fear, awaiting the next knock on the door."

If the leadership style of asset focusing works for someone who has to break the news to people that they are under arrest, it will work for you. Be like Lew's dad and condition yourself to see assets in the people you meet.

2. Be a "pick 'em up" type of person with everyone you meet. Grow into a leader and give people a lift by recognizing their assets.

3. Be a leader by developing the ability to see people's assets even in their liabilities. While working as a personnel consultant to a U.S. container drum company, Lew Losoncy would analyze personnel profiles to help the company make proper placements. At times, when the company was thinking of dismissing an employee, it was obvious that further evaluation was needed. Sometimes, an employee's liabilities in one department could become assets if he or she were to be placed in another department. Lew had a discussion with one stubborn employee named Mark, whose compulsive style was unyielding and whose inflexibility made it difficult for those who worked with him. At the time, the company was plagued with high insurance rates due to injuries in the plant. The plant sorely needed someone who could reverse the trend. "Why not put Mark in charge of safety?" the far-thinking division manager suggested.

In three years' time, with Mark in charge of safety, accidents dropped 35% and so did the company's insurance rates. The liability of stubbornness was, to an asset-focusing leader, turned into a positive success story. In his new position, Mark proved to be a top-notch employee.

The Fourth Skill Of A Leader: Developing Your Alternative Perceptions

Was Benedict Arnold an American traitor or a British hero? Has the computer helped or hindered society's development? Would allowing the laws of supply and demand to regulate the economy be the best approach to a sound fiscal policy?

These questions may inspire sparks among advocates of one side or the other. And while many people fight back and forth on these issues, the true leader is one who can stand above and beyond to take a higher level perspective on the issue. While most people's responses to these questions come from their own vantage points and are steered by their own needs, the leader is the one who can see both sides of the argument objectively and provide the alternate perspectives needed.

1. Be a leader by developing your perceptual alternatives. You have free will and can look at people and things from many vantage points. Practice this skill constantly. Try to look at people and issues that you face in many new ways. Think of the last time you had a disagreement with someone. Stop for a minute and try to get into the other person's shoes and convincingly present his or her position. If you can, you have taken a giant step toward developing your understanding and leadership style.

Glenn, a client of Lew's, was a very intelligent person. While Lew never administered any intelligence tests to Glenn, his best guess was that he was close to a genius. He had a bachelor's degree in economics and was well beyond his formal education in that discipline. Despite his ability and his education in economics, Glenn had difficulty finding employment. Glenn's older brother, a home builder, decided to make Glenn the head a four-man sales force. Along with supervising the four men, Glenn had sales responsibilities as well. He failed miserably and was quite frustrated in this role.

During a counseling session, it became obvious why this quite knowledgeable person was not "cutting the mustard." Glenn explained, "People are so stupid that they can't see how a home fights long-range inflation. I even take my college economics textbook to show them. I instruct them to read the book before we meet again. Do you know that very few people ever return?" Glenn's major error was in thinking that people perceive life as he does. All of his intelligence, his impressive background, and his knowledge actually worked against him because he didn't use them by starting off in the customer's world.

Lew's goal was to help Glenn develop the talent of perceptual alternatives. To achieve this end, they role-played. Lew asked Glenn to be a customer, and Lew was a skin and hair care consultant. (At the time, Lew was employed by a manufacturer of beauty products.) Glenn became confused with the highly technical language Lew employed. Lew instructed Glenn to read a highly technical book on the physiology of skin care and come back in a week to see him. At that time, they would talk about what Glenn had read. Glenn got the message. He now makes it a point to remind himself every day to perceive the world from the customer's perspective. Be a leader by developing your ways of seeing things from the other person's perspective.

2. Rise above the conflicts in your family or your organization by using perceptual alternatives.

One of the most interesting experiences Lew ever had was while serving as a consultant to a Pennsylvania school district. In this capacity, he had the opportunity to work with school board members, school administrators, teachers, custodians, students, and parents. He worked with each group on "How to Be Encouraging" and "How to Communicate More

Effectively." The length of the sessions with each group varied from three to thirty hours.

What insights Lew gained! All the groups in the organization had something in common. Each thought they were getting a raw deal. The board members, for example, felt that they were "unpaid scapegoats" and basically unappreciated. The school administrators felt that their hands were tied and they couldn't make any decisions that would rock the boat. The teachers blamed the school board for not caring, the administrators for not disciplining the students, and the children for not listening. The secondary school teachers even blamed the elementary school teachers for not preparing the children for high school. In turn, the elementary school teachers blamed the parents for their permissive child-rearing practices. The custodians criticized the administrators for not laying down the law in terms of cleanliness in the cafeteria and hallways. The janitors blamed the teachers and the students for not picking up after themselves in the classrooms. The students blamed the administrators for their tough, inflexible rules and accused many teachers of not caring and being interested only in getting their paychecks. The parents blamed the school board members for using their position as a stepping stone to gain political clout and blamed the administrators for punishing the children when the teachers were at fault. The parents also blamed the teachers for not teaching! Incredible, isn't it? Yet this same pattern of placing blame is present in every organization.

To deal with these organizational problems, Lew again used the technique of role playing. He said to the teachers, "Let's imagine that we are all school administrators. We are principals, and this is a principals' convention. Now, for one-half hour, let's think about all of the things we have to complain about." One teacher started, "Well, these teachers are always on my back to get rid of this annoying kid." Another teacher chimed in, "Yes, and the parents are never satisfied. They think that their child is the only one I have in school."

As time went on and the problems principals face were being discussed, the teachers walked a mile in the principals' shoes. They increased their vision and saw alternative ways of perceiving the principal's role. By rising above the conflict, it was not long before the members of the group gained appreciation for their teaching positions. They perceived the world from the alternative perspective and the grass was not greener on the other side. Develop your leadership style by doing the same. Rise above the conflict and use perceptual alternatives.

The Fifth Skill Of A Leader: Encouraging Team Spirit

1. Build team spirit by emphasizing cooperation as opposed to competition among members.   Observe an organization, a family, or any team with flaring spirit and strong morale, and you will find a talented leader in the picture. No doubt one talent the leader possesses is the ability to de-emphasize competition among teammates and put the accent on cooperation.

2. Build team power by giving group credit and encouraging each group member to do the same.   Talented leaders encourage the group, and they help each member to become an encourager as well. Donald Muzyka was such a talented leader. Dr. Muzyka, a divisional vice-president of the Carpenter Technology Corporation, is one of the top metallurgists in the world. In addition, he was a leader who put a great deal of energy into helping his five unique divisions work together.

Lew Losoncy was inspired by Dr. Muzyka's opening remarks in a lecture on team power given to his 400 divisional employees. The Ph.D. of metallurgy displayed an acute knowledge of human behavior when he recommended, "Look at the power we have when we work together." He cited no less than five specific instances in which cooperation among the five divisions achieved successful results.

Dr. Muzyka went on to tell a story about the power of teamwork, which he learned from his minister. As the story goes, a person was given the opportunity to observe the difference between Heaven and Hell. The person was first taken to Hell. There he observed a large banquet hall full of delicious foods, but no one could eat because their arms were extended straight out and they could not bend them to put the food in their mouths. "The frustration of Hell," he thought. "You can see the things you can't have. You are immobilized."

The observer was then taken to Heaven. To his amazement, he observed the same delicious food and the same unbending arms. But here, in Heaven, the people had figured out a way to eat. With their stiff arms, they faced each other and fed each other. Cooperation was the difference. It was cooperation that helped people achieve their goals.

3. Build team togetherness by sharing the similarities that you observe among group members.

When traveling in a foreign country, it is often refreshing to meet someone from your homeland. Maybe you have experienced even more of a coincidence by running into someone from your own city. If so, perhaps you talked about common experiences, people, or restaurants. Spotting similarities is a fast, sound, effective way to build a relationship.

Effective conversationalists, good psychotherapists, and successful leaders are able to find links with other people. This skill can be yours if you develop the ability to see similarities. It warms up a cold, distant relationship. There are countless potential links. Find the similarities.

4. Build team togetherness by being a common interest detective.

Observe team members in your family, your workplace, and your social or professional organizations and try to find common interests. Sports, movies, cars, books, and hobbies are just a few of the potential common interests that link people together. Become skilled at introducing two strangers by mentioning a subject that links them together. Because of your skill, they will be strangers for no more than a few seconds. Be a detective and find the common denominator among people.

5. Build a person-to-person link by identifying common struggles and challenges that face each person.

"John, you felt the same way about facing the bar exam, didn't you?"

> "I also went bankrupt a few years ago, and I thought I
> would never be in the black again. I could never have
> guessed that things would turn out this well."

Be a successful leader by linking people together through their
common struggles and challenges.

**6. Build team togetherness by emphasizing the common goal
that links the members of the team.**   Members of any organization have a similar link: achieving the goal of that organization. An
effective leader keeps pointing to that goal by creating a fast-holding
strong link:

> "This is the big game and we need the best from everyone.
> Guards and tackles, we need you to function as a high-
> powered blocking machine for our quarterback so he can
> get the passes to the receivers. With everyone doing his
> share for the team, we can win!"

Be a winning leader by transforming a few individuals into a
team through the power of linking. Look for common interests,
common challenges, and common goals.

**7. Build team morale by focusing on team effort, instead of
just success or failure.**   If you think about it, success is rarely the
result of one giant leap; rather, success is normally the product of
a series of efforts. The United States did not land a man on the moon
in one day. The achievement was the result of a series of plans,
trials, errors, and corrections. The effective leader knows that the
most important gift that individuals can give to the team is *effort.*
When people constantly give their effort, success will eventually
come, but if leaders focus only on success and failure, they may
discourage the individual and soon lose the person's effort.

The encouraging leader acknowledges the efforts of team members. Any effort in itself can be considered a success. Effort is a sign
of life. It is one of the most important resources that people have.

Be a "give-it-your-best-shot" person. Instead of asking, "Did you
make the swimming team?" ask, "Did you go out for the swimming

team?" Instead of asking, "Did you win top honors?" ask, "Did you give it a good shot?" Do the same with your total team. Build personal and team morale by focusing on effort instead of success or failure. Success is merely a result of an effective effort; failure is merely an indication that there is a better way and, with effort, you'll find it.

8. Emphasize the importance of improvement to team members to build realistic incentives and to "fire up" their efforts.   Help the person who failed the test to improve; assist the salesperson who had a devastating month to shoot for higher productivity; encourage the little girl who can count to three to try for four. Is there any limit to what can be achieved if a person keeps trying to do a little better today than yesterday?

Even the most effective and streamlined system in the world can be improved. Be wary of group members who want to keep things *status quo* or who fear change and improvement. Look for the person who has his or her eye on improvement. Keep team morale, team spirits, and team efforts high by encouraging everyone to think "bigger and better" and "more today than yesterday." Focus on improvement!

9. Be a successful leader by pointing out how each person is a necessary contributor to the goals of the team.   The need to contribute is powerful, as demonstrated during Lew Losoncy's visit to one first-grade classroom. All of the children but one were outside for recess. The little lad looked at Lew with bright eyes and asked, "Are you the man who helps the teachers?" "Yes," he responded. "Do you know what I gotta do this week, mister? When the kids run out for recess and don't push their chairs in, I gotta be the one who does it." The little lad was enthused about his job because he was contributing.

While working as a consultant to a publishing company which had low morale in many areas, especially the stockroom and order fulfillment departments, something interesting occurred to Lew. None of the employees really knew why they were there or why their contributions were significant.

Lew met with thirty-three of the clerks and stockroom employees. He asked each of them to consider that almost every book they mailed out went to an individual who, perhaps like themselves, waited for the mail to be delivered each day. Each book that the stockroom employees packaged each day had the potential to change lives—to change depression into joy, to change boredom into meaning in life. Lew congratulated them and asked that each person each day think about their contribution to the quality of people's lives!

Show group members how their unique contributions are a necessary part of the group's success. Show your children why going to school is important. Show your trash collector why you appreciate him or her. Show your mother and father how the meal they just carefully prepared is a meaningful contribution.

10. Build team togetherness and team spirit by celebrating together.   Frank Leidich was a master leader. As a supervisor, he would celebrate a productive season of mushroom growing by raising a glass of wine with his employees. Frank had his workers rise to give themselves a standing ovation. They couldn't wait for Victory Day.

Succeed with people by thinking like a leader and tapping the wealth of power on the team.

The Sixth Skill Of A Leader: Recognizing The Power Of Conveying Your Confidence In People

The philosopher Goethe argued that if you want someone to develop a trait, treat them as though they already have it. In their classic book *Pygmalion in the Classroom*, Robert Rosenthal and Lenore Jacobson wrote, "The self-fulfilling prophecy causes people, more often than not, to perform according to your expectations." As a leader, your confidence or lack of confidence in people actually is one of the most important factors in terms of how they will perform.

This phenomenon has been observed in numerous instances. Foremen have taken workers who others called incorrigible and turned them into productive people. Teachers have taken pupils labeled as "un-teachable" and helped them progress. Why? All because they had the power to convey their belief in the individual by communicating, "I know you can do it!"

George Vogel, the insightful director of the Council on Chemical Abuse in Berks County, Pennsylvania, is one of the top specialists in rehabilitating people with drug- and alcohol-related problems. George makes no bones about the importance of finding employers who show confidence in the abilities of former drug and alcohol addicts. George explained, "One of the most crucial decisions we make in our office is to find an employer who realistically faces the disease of alcohol and drug addiction. This employer must demand responsibility from the person going through rehabilitation. And on top of that, this special employer must be one who believes that the person can be responsible. If this confidence is conveyed to the rehabilitating person, our battle is halfway won."

Dig into your own experiences to see how this confidence works. Did you ever have a teacher or a supervisor who didn't have confidence in you? Everything that you did was put down. The harder you tried, the more this person focused on what went wrong. Eventually your performance level dropped and you became discouraged.

On the other hand, did you ever have a teacher, supervisor, or leader who truly believed in your abilities—who thought you were special—and conveyed this belief to you? What happened? In this situation, you were probably more creative, less anxious, and actually more productive.

1. Make a resolution every day to convey a fresh new confidence in the people around you.   Use this power of confidence to give people a new start. Treat them as though they had the trait you wish they had—and they soon will.

2. Be a leader by being the one person in the world who continues to believe in a person everyone else has given up on.

Application Of Positive Leadership Skills

Remember these tips for leadership:

1. Think your way to success the easy way: be a leader and enlist the help of everyone you know.

2. Observe leaders who make things happen and who achieve their goals. They are encouragers, not intimidators. Be a motivator of people, not a nit-picker. Encouragement is the key ingredient in effective leadership.

3. Be an encouraging **LEADER** by:

   Listening with full attention

   Empathizing with people

   Asset focusing

   Developing alternative perceptions

   Encouraging team spirit

   Recognizing the power of conveying confidence in people

Think Like A Leader Checklist

I. Leading Through Effective Communication
   A. Develop your skills in *attending* to other people's communications by:
      1. Using eye contact
      2. Having a relaxed, nondistracting body posture
      3. Staying on the topic of the conversation
      4. Striving for transmission of 100% of the message

   B. Develop your skills in *listening* to other people's communications by:
      1. Focusing on the feelings and emotions of others

    2. Targeting the concerns of others
    3. Developing the skill of nonjudgmental listening

  C. Develop your skills in *responding* to other people's communications by:
    1. Using "door openers" for further communication
    2. Avoiding "shoot and reload" dialogue
    3. Responding nonjudgmentally
    4. Demonstrating understanding of the other person's message

II. Motivating People Through Encouragement
  A. Develop your *responsibility* and *productivity* skills by:
    1. Focusing on efforts and contributions
    2. Recognizing resources, assets, and potentials
    3. Holding people responsible without blaming them
    4. Identifying subtle and not-so-subtle ways in which people are turned off
    5. Energizing personal enthusiasm for the concerns of others

  B. Develop your *respect* for others by:
    1. Conveying "I have confidence in your ability"
    2. Understanding the role of encourager expectations (self-fulfilling prophecy)
    3. Focusing on the interests of others
    4. Recognizing people's "claims to fame"
    5. Respecting people by "staying out of the way"
    6. Cooperating instead of competing with people
    7. Building relationships with mutual respect
    8. Recognizing the value of differences and the uniqueness in people

  C. Develop your skills in identifying *similarities* and sharing these links

  D. Develop your sense of *humor* in personal relationships

  E. Develop skills in assisting others to *overcome their discouraging ideas* by:

    1. Overcoming negative beliefs about yourself
    2. Overcoming negative beliefs about other people
    3. Overcoming negative beliefs about the world

F. Develop your skills in *establishing* short- and long-range *goals*

G. Develop your skills in mutually *evaluating progress* and movement toward goals

References

Losoncy, Lewis. *Teamwork Makes Our Dreamwork*. Solon, OH: Matrix Essentials, 1994.

Losoncy, Lewis. *The Motivating Team Leader*. Delray Beach, FL: St. Lucie Press, 1995.

Rosenthal, Robert and Lenore Jacobson. *Pygmalion in the Classroom*. New York: Holt, Reinhart, and Winston, 1968.

18 Self-Encouragement Skills

Bill is a positive, self-confident person. Those around him wonder how he got that way and, even more important, how he stays that way. Nothing ever seems to bother Bill. If it does, it's only for a short while, and then he's back into his positive emotional state.

If you followed Bill through a day, you would get an insight into how he became self-encouraging. Bill starts the day with some form of reasonably strenuous exercise (walking, running, or aerobics), which creates a flow of endorphins into his system. He also eats a diet that is focused on staying healthy instead of satisfying certain tastes. Every morning, he sits in a relaxed position with his eyes closed, takes deep breaths, and says positive phrases to himself. He comes out of these sessions with a positive outlook. He believes that this type of self-encouraging mental exercise is just as important as his physical exercise.

Bill avoids carrying blame, guilt, and self-accusation. He avoids sending himself discouraging messages and instead uses self-acceptance. He forgives himself. He does not carry around guilt because he believes he is already forgiven.

Bill often receives compliments from people at work and his friends. He accepts their compliments at face value. He doesn't reject them by saying, "Oh, anybody could have done that. It was nothing." Instead, he recognizes that he does things that merit affirmation and respect from others. He is not boastful about it; he is accepting.

As you become a more self-encouraging person, set up a systematic schedule that focuses on the self-encouragement process.

A discouraged person is a dependent person. As an encourager, you need to be more sensitive to the attempts of the discouraged person to become dependent upon you. It is essential in any relationship, whether at work or at home, that you refuse to take on the controlling role in that relationship. Instead, calmly, persistently, and in an encouraging manner, indicate you know the other person is responsible and can handle the situation.

To become a more encouraged person, you need to be in charge of your own self-respect and self-worth. In order to be a resource to others and increase their self-esteem, self-confidence, and feelings of worth, you first must feel positive about yourself.

How do people approach life? For some, a major goal is to feel happy, successful, and good about themselves (getting good grades in school, being recognized for accomplishments, having a good job, or earning lots of money). Their goal is simple—feeling worthwhile and feeling happy. The goal is accomplished by some external evaluation. You hear them say, "She made me sad (or angry)" or "He made my day, lifted me up, made me feel like I am really somebody."

While it is certainly positive and useful to be associated regularly with members of your family, business associates, or others who inspire you, what happens when you aren't around such people? This could be an excuse to feel discouraged, defeated, and not in control of your life.

When you are self-encouraging, you are able to help establish your own worth through self-validation. You don't wait for others to give you their approval. It is your own approval that is most important. You need to learn how to validate yourself. Validation is most effective when it comes from within. You are in charge of what is happening. You don't have to wait for someone else to create your feeling of validation. When you validate or encourage yourself, you are not comparing yourself to someone else by saying, "I'm the best athlete, the best musician, the most friendly..." Instead, you look at your traits; for example, you enjoy music, you like people, you are a good friend, or you are respected. None of these traits is comparative. There is no need to compare. Each of these traits is something you feel good about. When you stop thinking of life as a competition, race, or battle, you will then have more time to step back, recognize your own uniqueness, "smell the roses," and be more self-encouraging.

Self-encouragement is based on self-love. Unless we have self-love, we cannot be self-encouraging or encouraging to others. Robert Schuller, author of *Possibility Thinking,* a concept basic to being an encouraging person, has written extensively on the concept of self-love. In his book *Self-Love* (1969), he sets forth the following steps to a strong self-love:

1. Get rid of your fear of failure. The fear of failure only keeps you from moving forward. This keeps us from knowing and valuing ourselves.

2. Discover that unique person called you. Make this discovery by getting in touch with your hidden potential, in sharing, in being involved, and in being responsible.

3. Compliment yourself. This means you begin by investigating, verbalizing, and owning your strengths. What are the messages you typically program yourself with?
   "I'm a fool to let her treat me that way."
   "It was stupid to buy that car."
   "That was a dumb move."

Think of positive messages you can send yourself:
   "Joe is a good friend and respects me."
   "I am fun to be with."
   "People value my opinion."

Negative nonsense is based on the negative, self-destructive beliefs that you create and tell yourself.
"I'm not effective."
"Others are better than me. I don't have a chance."

How would you deprogram the negative nonsense you have been telling yourself and turn it into positive, valued messages?

As you become more aware of the negative nonsense you tell yourself, you also become aware that it is not other people who are discouraging you. It is *you* who discourages yourself with these negative messages.

To be more self-accepting, you need to learn to forgive yourself. Guilt is removed when you believe you are totally forgiven by God. Unfortunately, many of us continue to be critical of ourselves even though we have been forgiven. In this case, you need to be put in touch with how to affirm yourself. How do you usually respond to a positive comment? For example:

"I really appreciate your staying to do this typing."

"That was a great game you played!"

"Your acting (or singing) was so enjoyable."

If you want to know why you are having a hard time feeling good about yourself, you don't have to look far. Begin by looking in the mirror. Do you find it difficult to recognize your strengths, your qualities, and feel positive about yourself? Do you tend to flick off an affirmation by saying, "Oh, it was nothing." Do you look shyly at the ground and say, "Anybody could have done it." Do you feel embarrassed? All these responses are affirmation flicks. They treat the affirmation as an insect that needs to be quickly brushed off the body. If you are to be self-encouraging and increase your self-respect and self-worth, learn to appreciate yourself and to accept the validation of others. Then you might respond differently.

"I really appreciate your staying to do this typing."
"I enjoy staying to work on something important."

"That was a great game you played!"
"Thanks, I thought I was really 'on' my game."

"Your acting (or singing) was so enjoyable."
"Thanks, acting (or singing) is something I enjoy doing well."

There are two major ways to establish worth and value: extrinsic and intrinsic. The extrinsic way comes through the feedback we receive from others and from the things we possess. Extrinsic value may come from praise, recognition, salary or income, a house, a car, and the like. Unfortunately, these are all temporary and can change at any time. If our friends and boss stop praising us, if we fail to get public recognition for a performance, or if we lose some of our major possessions, we may begin to experience lack of self-worth.

The problem with extrinsic value and worth is that you have absolutely no control over it. You are totally subject to the faulty beliefs of others. You believe that their opinions are more important than your own.

Intrinsic value, on the other hand, comes from focusing on your internal evaluation. You do not set competitive standards or comparisons with others. If you are satisfied with the way you are functioning, comparisons become irrelevant.

Intrinsic value is important in the sense that you are able to be in control of the evaluation process. It would be foolish for someone who owns a store to let the customers determine the price of the goods or materials that were sold. However, when you are subject to extrinsic valuation, you are basically doing the same thing. Instead of asking "How are you?" you ask "How am I?" or worse, "Am I okay? Am I worthwhile? Do you like me? How can I change myself to fit your needs?"

When you are intrinsically motivated, you are able to focus on your own efforts, contributions, and assets. If you improve your skill in a sport, for instance, you can feel good about that regardless of any comparison to others, knowing that you are making a full effort. As you are intrinsically motivated, you have a wider perspective on life. You can see the real value of effort, contribution, and involvement. You don't suffer from tunnel vision (being enthusiastic only about excellence, being at the top, making major contributions or super efforts). Joy comes into your life without the need to compare. The little things in life count as big things.

Can you differentiate how the extrinsically motivated and the self-encouraged person would react to the following events?

Winning the first round of a tournament

Winning the tournament

Getting a five-dollar raise

Being given five new sales prospects

Receiving a call from a friend he or she hasn't heard from in some time

Being invited to help clean the church

It is important that evaluations come from within you to enable you to be more encouraging to yourself. Internal evaluation occurs when you listen to the messages inside you in order to establish and increase your self-worth.

Exercises For Self Encouragement And Increasing Self-Worth

1. Sit comfortably in a relaxed position and close your eyes. Take a few deep breaths and say the following simple phrase to yourself: "I love myself unconditionally." Pause for about five seconds and then repeat the phrase three times.

   You may become aware of some resistance, hurts, and self-constrictions you have regarding self-encouragement and self-love.

2. This exercise is best done with a partner. You will talk and the other person will listen. Standing comfortably, with your arms relaxed at your side, make eye contact. Say to your partner, "I love myself unconditionally." Pause. Take several relaxed breaths and repeat the phrase.

   What's going on inside you? What kind of growth are you

experiencing? What kind of fears and constrictions do you have?

3. In this exercise, relax, take a deep breath, and identify some place in your life that is beautiful and relaxing, a place where you are more positive by being there. Visualize this place and feel it in your body. See it, hear the sounds, smell the smells, feel all the sensory sensations. Feel the love you have for this place, and get a clear picture of all the sensations. Once you have this clear feeling of love in your mind, direct the feeling of love toward yourself instead of feeling it toward the place (Hendricks, 1990).

The Self-Encouraged Person Applications

As you develop the skill of self-encouragement, you will begin to move in the following directions:

1. You will make choices and take responsibility for your choices. Instead of acting as if your situation is out of your hands, or is your destiny, you will become involved in creating your world through personal choices. What happens to you is a result of your choices, and you take responsibility for them. If you are out of condition, the cause is lack of conditioning; if you are overweight, the cause is your diet and lack of exercise.

    Identify a situation you think is out of your control and believe there is nothing you can do about it.

    What new choice can you make?

2. Trust your own evaluations of the world. Instead of depending on others' appraisals of persons or things, create your own values. You may have evaluated friends on the basis of

their titles, degrees, or money. Now you are free to see them as they are, without any external status. When you learn to trust your own evaluations of the world, you lift the oppressive chains of "I wonder what other people will think."

What is something you have trusted to the evaluations of others?

How can you reevaluate this?

3. As you become more self-encouraged, you become more independent of others' opinions. We are often dependent on what others think about our clothing, car, place of residence, job title, hobbies, and beliefs. When you begin to believe that your opinion is as good as the opinions of others, you are further encouraged. As you come to believe that what you think is more important for you than always deferring to what others think, you are free to grow and, equally important, free to encourage others.

    In what areas have you been overly influenced by the opinions of others?

    How can you come to trust your opinion on something specific?

4. As you become more self-encouraging, you are better able to disagree when appropriate. The person heavily influenced by others lacks the courage to stand up for his or her own opinion. Disagreeing involves seeing a discrepancy or incongruency in another's opinion and being willing to assert your own opinion. Suppose you are in a group where people

make negative remarks about an ethnic or religious group. Your experience does not coincide with theirs. Now you must decide whether to give in to the majority opinion or stand up for what you believe. As you learn to say what you believe, you will find yourself tremendously encouraged.

A friend states an opinion on some issue about which you are informed. You believe exactly the opposite of what he or she has expressed. What will you say?

5. As you become more encouraged, you have less need for special attention, power, getting even, or displaying inadequacy. Instead, you will seek to increase your social interest by involvement and contributing. Your self-esteem will come from being more autonomous and responsible. You will become concerned with equality and justice and have a willingness to participate in the give and take of life.

Pick a specific situation and show how you can react differently by moving from self-interest to social interest and by moving from being discouraged to being encouraged.

How To Turn A Discouraged Behavior Into An Encouraging Behavior

6. The self-encouraging person is a risk taker. This doesn't mean attempting things that are foolish. Instead, the self-encouraging person is courageous in making an effort even though the performance may not be good. The joy of participating is more important than what others will think. A risk taker is willing to try things that may not be completely successful. Unlike some people who do not try athletics, music, art, or other activities for fear of looking bad, the risk taker is less concerned with looks and more concerned with involvement.

What are some things you do not participate in because you think you will look bad or won't do well?

How can you change the faulty beliefs that keep you from taking a risk?

What is a more courageous belief which will help you become a risk taker?

7. The self-encouraged person perceives the alternatives to any situation. The person who believes "I'm only alright if I get a raise in pay every year" limits himself or herself by failing to recognize that although not getting a raise is unfortunate, it does not mean failure. This person is able to tap into many other areas of life—social, musical, athletic, emotional, behavioral—where he or she is a success.

Self-encouragement is essential to becoming an encouraging person. When you are able to encourage yourself, you have found a precious jewel. Like the early explorers who struggled to find gold, you have located your own gold— yourself. Take stock of your positive traits (friendliness, intelligence, helpfulness, concern, willingness to share). Make these traits visible, and do not engage in comparisons with others. As you learn to accept, value, and spotlight your assets, it becomes easier for you to do the same for others.

References

Hendricks, Gay. *The Learning to Love Yourself Workbook.* NY: Fireside Book/Simon & Schuster, 1990.

Schuller, Robert. *Move Ahead with Possibility Thinking.* New York: Jove Inspiration, 1967.

Schuller, Robert. *Self-Love: The Dynamic Force of Success.* New York: Hawthorn Books, 1969.

19

Living As A Courageous, Positive Person

The word *courage* is often misunderstood in our society. We tend to think of courage as it relates to athletic heroes, leaders of business and industry, or the person who faces a difficult relationship or illness in a brave manner. All these people face challenges, but courage means more than facing challenges. The courageous person has heart and hope in facing daily problems.

Courageous people have beliefs that direct the way they meet the challenges of life. Whether at work, in social relationships, or elsewhere, courageous people approach their challenges on the basis of their beliefs. The courageous person believes, "I can do it. Give me a chance. I will do my best. Let the chips fall where they may." This person communicates a clear belief in self and a willingness and ability to make an effort and be productive. Courageous people do not feel they need to take risks in everything. They take a chance for causes that they consider to be worthwhile.

You may be wondering, "Am I a courageous person?" There are several guidelines to help you answer that question.

1. You have a clear goal that guides the actions you take in the major situations in your life. If you have no goals, it is very difficult to tell whether you are succeeding or failing. As a matter of fact, this may be one of the ways you protect yourself from failing. No goal equals no achievement. Nothing ventured equals nothing lost and no achievement missed.

2. You act decisively once you determine that a risk is worth taking and it appears to be appropriate to move ahead promptly.

3. You accept the fact that you may make mistakes, that everything doesn't have to be done perfectly. It is highly unlikely that a courageous person will not make mistakes. Are you ready to accept yourself, even with mistakes? Are you ready to accept mistakes as a part of life? If you never experience mistakes, then most likely you are not taking any chances to help you grow. No mistakes can often be translated into no progress.

4. Do you know your limits? Do you know when it is not sensible for you to move ahead?

5. Do you avoid blaming others? Do you accept responsibility? The basic premise for the courageous person is that *everyone is responsible but no one is to blame.* As a courageous person, you accept responsibility for your actions. You aren't interested in finding somebody to blame. Our ego usually leads us to point to somebody else as being at fault. If you are going to be courageous, stop blaming and accept responsibility.

How does courage, or the lack of courage, affect your daily life? Start with a specific area, like your job or the place where you spend a considerable amount of time. Ask yourself the following questions: "If I had more courage, what would I do about my work? Would I plan differently? Would I spend my time at work more intensively and then have more extended periods of recreation and leisure? Would I take more time to enjoy the parts of my work that are really fun?" The courageous person lives life to the fullest.

At this point you may be thinking, "This sounds good, but what do I do about the mortgage, my children's education, my responsibilities, my relationships, my parents, my debts...?" If you have courage, you might consider looking at these concerns differently. You might decide that living courageously could provide all the rewards necessary to be a fully satisfied person. Take a courageous look at the many excuses that keep you from being satisfied. They may not be responsibilities. Instead, they may be your lack of willingness to let go of your excuses.

Courage helps you become a more autonomous, responsible, decisive individual. In your work and in your relationships, you may be asked to do things you feel others should be responsible for or others might do better. Yet the reality remains—either you do it or it will not get done. The courageous person does it anyway by taking responsibility for what needs to be done.

You can increase your courage by becoming aware of the stumbling blocks that hinder you from becoming more courageous in your work, relationships, and friendships. In some instances this is done by engaging in counseling or psychotherapy to get in better touch with your own beliefs, values, attitudes, and goals, which really direct your daily life. Your decision to be courageous is rather simple. You either develop, possess, and own courage and then eventually act upon it, or you function as a fearful, discouraged person. People who do not believe in themselves do not believe they "can do it." They don't even make an attempt to try.

The Courage To Be Imperfect

The courage to be imperfect is an important concept developed by Dr. Rudolf Dreikurs, an internationally known psychiatrist. Dreikurs suggested that we may continuously pursue perfection without any hope of obtaining it. To establish a high standard of competitiveness and over-ambition in ourselves and our children, we expect ourselves to be better or more. It is almost as if we wear a T-shirt that reads, "I'm not as much as I should be, but I'm working on it." Many of us might think that's an appropriate sentiment, but let's really think about it. In essence, we are advertising that we do not believe we are enough just as we are. That simply isn't true! Everyone is unique and distinctly different from any other human being on the face of the earth. We have everything we potentially need to be effective. The problem is in recognizing our potential and having the courage to use it.

One factor that puts us in a discouraging mode is our over-concern with self-elevation, or prestige. Ask yourself some simple questions to check this out: Am I concerned about whether I am better than others? Does it bother me that others make more money than I do? Do I want the most expensive house or automobile? These comparisons eventually lead to discouragement and dissatisfaction.

Consider society's attitude about mistakes. Mistakes can be dangerous and are to be avoided at all costs. However, look at a group of youngsters playing basketball on a playground. They take each mistake as an opportunity to learn a more effective way to shoot the basketball. The same children in the classroom may have an intense teacher who puts a lot of pressure on them to be perfect. Whatever the result, it is a learning opportunity.

Many of our human relationships are mistake-centered. Some people take extreme pleasure in pointing out the mistakes of others. They are under the faulty assumption that this makes them better than others. If you are the one who made the mistake and I didn't, then obviously there is something superior about me—or is there? People who have the courage to be imperfect are willing to try things regardless of the result. They develop a sense of their own strength and worth. They have a feeling of self-acceptance and avoid the pressures of competition, unrealistically high standards, and over-ambition, which tend to create discouragement.

The courage to be imperfect is an important trait. Own it. Embrace it. Live it, and then give it to those around you who need it most.

Courage

Courage displays itself in our willingness to take on challenges and to see obstacles as opportunities to succeed. Courage also shows itself in our ability to say yes when we are needed as well as our ability to say no when we recognize that something is not in our best interest.

People often encounter challenges to their courage, such as the ability to take a stand for what they believe in. If it is important to belong, to be accepted, to be a part of the group, then what do you do when you are asked to do something that doesn't fit with your values or standards? The capability to say no and stand up for what you believe is courage. When you really believe in yourself, have high self-esteem, and believe you are someone worthwhile, then you are comfortable being courageous.

The person with courage can look at a situation or event and see possible actions and solutions instead of just the dangers. Courageous people proceed without hesitation and meet the challenges that exist in life. They don't back off. Instead, they move forward courageously. Courage is not to be confused with reckless behavior, however. A reckless person takes chances, but the reckless act only appears to be courageous. A courageous person always expresses an underlying conviction of positive emotions and beliefs.

Courage and fear are actually very similar. In reality, they are both based on how you think about things. Fear is obviously negative, directed against, rather than for, something. Courage, instead, is positive. It can be direct and active. Both courage and fear are based on the valuation of self and the situation. One is a positive evaluation; the other is a negative evaluation.

Courage is the confidence one possesses in oneself and one's ability to cope with any situation that may arise. It is a conviction that you can work to find a solution you can cope with any predicament you are facing.

Courage is the opposite of fear. The potential for courage is always present. It is a matter of your perception. Courage is:

- Saying yes to yourself
- Facing opportunities and challenges
- Recognizing and affirming any slight progress on your part
- Building your self-esteem
- Cooperation and win/win relationships
- Faith and believing, standing up for your values, integrity, and involvement

Courage is saying yes to yourself instead of referring to others. When you say yes to yourself, you recognize that your needs, goals, and priorities are important. This small step of courage increases your self-esteem and self-worth. It need not be offensive or obnoxious to others. It simply indicates that you are important. You believe in yourself and the things you strive to accomplish.

Courage says yes to your values and your worth, as you value yourself and look forward to situations that are positive and produce growth. Courage says yes to an opportunity when someone presents you with an idea, a chance to do something different, or an opportunity to move ahead, even though you have some doubts. Courage gives you the opportunity to speak out with a very firm "yes." Courage is found in your movement or any kind of effort that clearly shows you are making progress. Courage is shown in risking, caring, and, more important, believing.

The courageous person is not afraid to take a chance for something that is of value and makes a difference. The courageous person is one who cares and is willing to express his or her feelings. A courageous person isn't afraid to say, "I miss you" or "I love you" or "I need you." Courageous people don't hide their feelings within themselves, but rather are willing to share them. They recognize that sharing their feelings is not a sign of weakness but a sign of strength. They participate actively in life instead of seeing it as a spectator sport. There is just no way you can grow without taking a chance.

David Viscott (1977) expressed this very succinctly in the following words:

> If you cannot takes risks on your own behalf, you are not your own person.
> You are your biggest problem.
> If you cannot risk, you cannot grow.

The Development Of Courage

No decision or value judgment is more important than the decision to develop courage. Seeing yourself as courageous and willing to take a risk and try, instead of being discouraged, influences all your interactions and satisfactions. The single most significant key to your behavior and your self-esteem is the development of courage. When you are courageous, you have self-respect and a sense of your own worth and value. You are able to choose your actions. You accept yourself, and you are able to act upon your decisions. When you have confidence, you choose goals that are aligned and fit with your actions. Complete the following phrase.

If I had more courage, I would...

Did you have the courage to complete the sentence, or did you quickly skip to the next paragraph? That's a basic problem with courage. The only place you can find it is inside yourself.

Suppose have a problem dealing with the demands of others, and this often puts you in an uncomfortable position. The following simple imagery exercise can strengthen your courage.

Focus on any unwarranted or unreasonable request from a person to whom you generally say yes but have wanted to say no. Picture yourself being asked to do something and firmly declining by saying no. Practice this several times a day. As you picture yourself saying no and doing it in a firm, tactful way, you become in touch with certain feelings and tensions. As you get in touch with these tensions, become aware of other images that begin to emerge as you firmly decline. Take a moment to practice visualizing.

The following exercises will give you an opportunity to become more aware of your beliefs and your courage. Read each sentence and record the first thing that comes to mind.

Work:

If I had more courage at work, I would...

When I don't show courage at work, I am...

Friendship:

If I had more courage with my friends, I would...

If I were a courageous person, my friends would...

If I had more courage, I wouldn't watch life go by; instead I would...

If I had more courage, I'd let people know how I really feel by...

Leisure:
If I had more courage, I'd spend more time in activities I enjoy, such as...

If I had more courage, I'd do these activities regularly by...

The route to courage isn't found on the main streets and the main highways. The route to courage is often through the side streets and small roads. It is there because it is seldom used and the path is not very worn.

In some instances you may doubt that you have courage. Don't doubt it. The courage is there. It only needs to be brought out into the light. You can bring it out by setting up a very simple system. Look at the areas of your life that you want to do something about and identify examples of courageous actions. Do a minimum of one of these activities each day.

Characteristics Of A Courageous Person

A courageous person:

- Is concerned with the needs of others
- Welcomes the unknown and unexpected
- Believes in self and has no need to have others prove his or her worth
- Is capable of internal control

Beliefs And Behavior Of A Courageous Person

A courageous person believes in himself or herself. While courageous people are open to new ideas and beliefs and give serious considerations to alternate viewpoints, in the end they take full responsibility for their decisions.

This self-trust enables a courageous person to enjoy making decisions. A person who is afraid of making mistakes looks to others to take responsibility. A courageous person sees decision making and responsibility as proof that he or she is alive and significant. When their decisions prove ineffective, courageous people don't shift the blame to others, but rather seek a more effective solution in case the problem occurs again in the future. If they believe the same situation will not happen again, they even avoid pondering the matter. Thus, they are practical, realistic, and independent.

With this self-trust, courageous people have little need to be approved of by others. Their source of satisfaction is internal as opposed to external. It means they will not compromise what they trust for the sake of the approval and acceptance of others. Thus, while they have many *wants* in their relationships with others, they have few *needs*! Consequently, courageous people, as opposed to dependent people, don't spend their time apologizing for their lives; instead, they live their lives responsibly.

This independence and self-trust enable courageous people to stand up against even a majority while supporting the position they believe in. If they state their position, they do so without the emotional involvement exhibited by some ego-involved people. They just present their perceptions and expect the other person to do the same.

Courageous people do not turn to "experts" for direction on how to live their lives. What is right for them, they believe, can only be answered by them. They don't need to read a book on etiquette in order to act appropriately.

They trust themselves and their inner judgments. They even resist the traditional "shoulds" of their culture (eating three meals a day, getting eight hours of sleep, always deferring to others) if they believe these rule makes no sense to them. Courageous people are sometimes viewed as nonconformists. This is not really the case, because they conform when conformity makes sense. Their resistance is not based upon rejection of authority; it is based on rejection of ideas that are meaningless to them.

The more discouraged a person is, the greater the need to distort or deny what they experience in life. If someone has a need to be perfect, for example, and fails at a task, the failure is resolved by blaming it on someone else. A person who has a need to be liked by everyone and is rejected can fool himself or herself by saying that the other person is worthless and their opinion doesn't count.

This need to distort reality to fit the wishes of the person does not exist in the courageous person. A courageous person has the ability to size up a situation and recognize what is real and what can and cannot be changed—and gets started.

Courageous people recognize the difference between *what exists* and what they *wish would exist*. They respect people too much to demand that others adjust to their opinions. Once you trust in yourself, you become accepting of not only self but of others. You are able to see people as they are more clearly instead of how you would prefer them to be. You are also more aware of your own strengths and weaknesses. You recognize the difference between the facts and someone else's opinion of the facts.

Being Open To Experiences

Complaining about "what if" is futile and counterproductive. The more discouraged a person is, the more closed he or she is to new ideas and viewpoints. A discouraged person has limited perceptions and divides the world into dualistic compartments of right and wrong, good and bad. This simplifies life because the person doesn't have to choose or decide.

Maslow (1954) believed that this quality of openness was related to healthy people being "problem centered" as opposed to "ego centered." When people are ego centered, their energies are focused on self and on defending the self that exists at that time. Essentially, closed-mindedness is the generalized omnipotent feeling that where

I am now is absolutely correct and any change on my part would then necessarily be incorrect. For ego-centered people to change would mean that they were originally wrong. And the ego-centered person associates being wrong with having less worth.

With a growing, open-minded, and problem-centered attitude, courageous people have no need to defend a position. They see their viewpoint as simply being the best available to them at that moment, and as the information changes, perhaps their position will also.

Developing Social Interest In Humankind

The more discouraged a person is, the greater his or her need to compete, be one up, seek power, and manipulate others. For a discouraged person, life is a game, and the game is played not only to win but to see that others lose. When others lose, a discouraged person is temporarily distracted from his or her own weaknesses and limitations.

Courageous people are comfortable in the world. They have social interest. Feelings of being united to humanity know no geographical boundary. Loyalty, to courageous people, is directed toward everyone regardless of whether they are of the same nationality, religion, or even family. Courageous people cut through artificial barriers.

Being rooted in people gives courageous people meaning in life, and that meaning becomes fulfilled through encouraging others. Their desire to contribute is strong. They seek cooperation and mutual respect as opposed to competition in their relationships with people. They are also sensitive to how others perceive the world. By rejecting the role of title, prestige, and material wealth in human relationships, a courageous person values people above position.

Developing Increased Personal Responsibility

Discouraged people function as if they are passive and helpless victims of their past, other people, and life. By claiming helplessness, they receive the fringe benefits of having an excuse for their lack of involvement and personal responsibility.

Their lifestyle is woven with the theme of "If only it weren't for...I could move ahead." When the causes for their behavior lie outside themselves, it follows that responsibility for their growth also lies outside themselves.

Courageous people, on the other hand, take full responsibility for their thoughts, feelings, and actions. They see no purpose in blaming others or the world for how they feel, think, or act. They courageously take the facts at the moment and energetically try to make changes. Their responsible attitude is even reflected in their language. They are more likely to say "I will" or "I choose not to" instead of "I can't." They feel alive and powerful and actively plan their goals and move toward them. They don't wait for the meaning of their life to arrive with the mailman or a phone call. Rather, they recognize the role they play in creating life's meaning.

The following outline shows the movement and differences between being courageous and being discouraged. Through encouragement, a person tends to adopt some of the feelings and actions listed on the right side.

Five areas where change may be observed are: (1) the courageous way of looking at reality, (2) the courageous way of looking at other people, (3) the courageous way of looking at yourself, (4) the courageous way of looking at new ideas and experiences, and (5) the courageous way of speaking (Maslow, 1954).

Being Courageous

The courageous way of *looking at reality* involves moving

from...	*to...*
1. **Demanding** that reality be different from fact: "People shouldn't have to die."	1. **Accepting** as facts of life those things that can't be changed: "Death is an inevitable part of life and I'm glad to have the opportunity to live."

2. **Demanding** that the world be easier than the way it is (demanding magic):
   "It shouldn't be this hard for me to lose weight."

2. **Facing the fact** that the world is the way it is and that reaching one's goals requires hard work:
   "Losing weight for me is hard, demanding work. It is worth my effort, however, to achieve the results."

3. **Passively waiting** for the world to change:
   "Someday I know the right person for me will come along."

3. **Actively** making changes in one's life:
   "I'm going out as often as I can to meet people."

4. **Demanding** that reality be fair:
   "It's unfair! All of my brothers and sisters are so attractive and look at me."

   "Why is it my friend can eat all the cake she wants and doesn't gain weight and I just look at food and put on pounds?"

4. **Realizing** that the world is not fair and adjusting to it:
   "It doesn't matter one bit how my brothers and sisters look."
   "What does matter is how I look and what I can do with myself to make myself more appealing."

5. Believing that **reality and the world must adjust to my wishes**:
   "I must win the lottery today. I need the money."

5. Understanding that **reality and the world are disinterested in what I wish**. Rather, it is my job to adjust to reality and the world:
   "I have a one in one thousand chance of winning the lottery, whether I need the money or not."

6. **Twisting** facts to fit my selfish needs:
   "It's my birthday, so I deserve the cake and ice cream even though I'm on a diet."

6. **Facing facts** regardless of my needs:
   "My diet doesn't give a hoot about what day it is when I count calories."

7. Using my energies to **gripe** about the way things are

7. Using my energies to **change** what I can and **accept** what I can't

8. Feeling **hopeless** and **helpless** about my circumstances in life: "Why wasn't I born into a family with money? There's just no sense trying to get ahead, since everything is stacked against me."

8. Feeling thrilled **by being alive** and realizing that I have a **lot of different ways of looking at and acting in my life**: "Where am I in life and where do I want to go? I have a lot of alternatives as long as I have life."

The courageous way of *looking at other people* involves moving

from...	*to...*
1. Believing that other people **should be and should act the way I want them to**	1. Believing that people **can be the way they choose**
2. The need to **manipulate others** through pity, depression, or force: "Look at what you have done to me. You have made me depressed."	2. Desiring to be **honest and genuine with others** without playing games: "I don't like what you did. But only I can make myself depressed."
3. More or less believing that other people are either stronger or weaker than I, so that some people must take over the responsibility of others	3. Believing that other people **are equal** to me—I do not have their responsibilities and they do not have mine
4. **Judging people** on the basis of income, nationality, clothing, etc. **before getting to know them**: "Isn't he Irish? I'll bet he must have a temper." "That person wears a beard. He must be a rebel."	4. Getting to know people as **individuals** regardless of their role or physical appearance: "He's Irish." "He has a beard."
5. Believing that **I need** the approval and acceptance of everyone to survive	5. Believing that while I **would like** everyone to like me, it is impossible

6. Believing that I should **timidly sacrifice my rights as a martyr for others**

7. Believing that **other people should be martyrs** and sacrifice their rights and time **for me**

8. Thinking that **my** opinions are **more important** than the opinions of other people

9. Believing that **the more I humiliate people, the more they respect me**

6. Believing that I have just as much right as anyone else and that I **want my fair share**. Being a martyr helps neither them nor me.

7. Recognizing that **other people have just as much right to their lives as I do to my life**

8. Accepting every person's opinion as important to them, even though I may agree or disagree

9. Recognizing that the more I focus on people's strengths and positive points, the better my relationship with them will be

The courageous way of *looking at yourself* involves moving

from...	*to...*
1. Believing that I can't change	1. Believing that although change is hard for me, I can change with courage
2. Thinking that feeling guilty about my past is helpful	2. Recognizing that guilt is an unproductive excuse for not changing. I am going to become determined and not feel guilty.
3. Feeling terrible every time I make a mistake	3. Appreciating mistakes as a natural part of growing. I am going to develop the courage to be imperfect.
4. Thinking that I have to be what other people want me to be	4. Becoming what I want to be regardless of others who try to force me into their mold
5. **Blaming** self, others, or the world	5. **Taking personal responsibility for my life**

6. **Living in the past**

7. **Hating myself**

8. Thinking that **my worth as a human being depends** on how much I make or who I am

9. **Worrying about** all kinds of catastrophes and what could occur **in the future**

10. Feeling that I only have negative points and am worthless

6. **Living in the present**

7. Liking myself

8. Recognizing that **I have worth just because I exist**

9. **Taking life in the present** and facing problems as they arrive

10. Becoming aware of how **complex I am, with strengths and weaknesses**

The courageous way of
looking at new ideas and experiences involves moving

from...	*to...*
1. Immediately **rejecting** new ideas just because they are not consistent with my current beliefs	1. Being open to new ideas as possible sources of growth
2. Seeing newness as a **threat**	2. Seeing newness as an **opportunity**
3. **Agreeing** with ideas **just because** they are held by friends, relatives, or any group	3. Agreeing with new ideas when they make sense to me
4. Seeking **sameness** on the job, eating the same foods, vacationing at the same spot, etc.	4. Seeking out new experiences in life
5. **Living every day** in the **same way**	5. Living every day in new exciting ways

The courageous way of *speaking* involves moving

from...	*to...*
1. "I can't"	1. "I will"

2. "Things **shouldn't** or **mustn't** be this way"

2. "I **would prefer that things** wouldn't be this way. But just because I prefer it doesn't mean they shouldn't be."

3. "I am this way"

3. "In my past, I was this way"

4. "They say..."

4. "I say..."

5. "I could never..."

5. "I am going to succeed at..."

6. All or none

6. Some

7. Horrible, awful, terrible, or catastrophic

7. Unfortunate or inconvenient

References

Maslow, A. *Motivation and Personality*. NY: Harper & Row, 1954.

Viscott, David. *Risking*. NY: Pocketbooks, 1977.